Why It's **Hard** To Be **Good**

Al Gini

Routledge
Taylor & Francis Group
New York   London

Published in 2006 by
Routledge
Taylor & Francis Group
270 Madison Avenue
New York, NY 10016

Published in Great Britain by
Routledge
Taylor & Francis Group
2 Park Square
Milton Park, Abingdon
Oxon OX14 4RN

© 2006 by Taylor & Francis Group, LLC
Routledge is an imprint of Taylor & Francis Group

Printed in the United States of America on acid-free paper
10 9 8 7 6 5 4 3 2 1

International Standard Book Number-10: 0-415-97263-9 (Hardcover)
International Standard Book Number-13: 978-0-415-97263-5 (Hardcover)
Library of Congress Card Number 2005014297

Library of Congress Cataloging-in-Publication Data

Gini, Al, 1944-
  Why it's hard to be good / Al Gini.
     p. cm.
  Includes bibliographical references and index.
  ISBN 0-415-97263-9 (hardback : alk. paper)
  1. Ethics. 2. Conduct of life. 3. Good and evil.   I. Title.

BJ1531.G53 2005
170--dc22   2005014297

Taylor & Francis Group
is the Academic Division of Informa plc.

Visit the Taylor & Francis Web site at
http://www.taylorandfrancis.com

and the Routledge Web site at
http://www.routledge-ny.com

To my muse and partner:

Sherry

"The study of philosophy is not that we may know what men have thought, but what the truth of things is."

—**Thomas Aquinas**

"Just as medicine confers no benefit, if it does not drive away physical illness, so philosophy is useless if it does not drive away suffering of the mind."

—**Epicurus**

"Reading should be an education of the heart . . . [It] reminds you that there is more than you, better than you."

—**Susan Sontag**

Contents

Prologue

Morals are an acquirement—like music, like a foreign language,
like piety, poker, paralysis—no man is born with them.

—Mark Twain

We need each other. We are not herd animals, but we are communal creatures. We are dependent on each other to survive and thrive. Good choices or bad choices, our collective existence requires us to continually make choices about "what we ought to do" in regard to others. Like it or not, we are by definition moral creatures. Ethics is primarily a communal, collective enterprise, not a solitary one. It is the study of our web of relationships with others. As a communal exercise, ethics is the attempt to work out the rights and obligations we have and share with others.

Defining ethics is not difficult. Living ethically is. At its most basic level, Episcopalian Archbishop Frank Griswald's definition of ethics is right: "Ethics is about the rules we choose to live by once we decide we want to live together." Sounds simple, but it isn't! Why? Because ethics requires us to be concerned about the rights and well-being of others. It requires us to stop thinking of ourselves as the sole center of the universe. It requires us to transcend the simplistic equation of "me, myself, and I." It requires us to be just, reasonable, and objective. It requires us to do something we do not want to do—be our best rational selves in regard to others.

Being obsessively preoccupied with self seems to be an elemental piece of the human psyche. It seems, if you will, to be part of our hardwiring. Some evolutionary biologists argue that self-absorption, self-centeredness, evolved out of our need to focus on self to help guarantee survival. From an evolutionary standpoint, preoccupation with self is both a defensive posture and an offensive tactic. It is about getting enough. It is about security and strength. It is about taking big bites. It is about not being part of someone else's food chain. It is about always looking at the world from the inside out. It is about measuring everything by one's own wants and needs. It is about being oblivious to the needs of others. It is about being concerned with others only when it is in your own best interest. It is about measuring everything by one's own wants and needs.

I believe that the central problem of ethics today is not a lack or moral reasoning or moral imagination but, rather, a lack of moral engagement. By that I mean a willingness to take on ethical issues and questions, a willingness to extend ourselves, a willingness to put ourselves in harm's way because we are concerned about the well-being of others. I think that we have forgotten a fundamental Socratic lesson: the goal of life is not to escape death, suffering, or inconvenience. The goal is to escape doing wrong and to live well with others.

Publicly, we may live lives that are economically and electronically interconnected and interdependent, but privately we are emotionally and ethically withdrawn, unappreciative, and unempathetic to the wants, needs, and desires of others. Cultural anthropologist Ernest Becker has argued that human nature is doomed to recapitulate the tragic failing of Narcissus. We live our lives hopelessly absorbed with self. If we care about anyone else at all, it is only after we have first taken care of our own self-centered wants and needs.

A - C - E

Futurists suggest that an atmosphere for creativity requires Talent, Technology/Tools, and Tolerance.

Ethicists suggests that an atmosphere for ethics requires A-Awareness of others; C-Care and concern for the well-being of others; E-Energy and the willingness to respond to the needs of others.

The central thesis and metaphor of this book is that people find it hard to do the right thing because they find it hard to stand outside the shadow of self. I believe that ethics (doing the right thing for the right reason and purposefully) is possible only when we are able to step away from ourselves or, to borrow a phrase, "to forget about ourselves on purpose." We must be able to see beyond our self-contained universe of personal concerns. We must be able to become, if only momentarily, more selfless than selfish.

Søren Kierkegaard said that "subjectivity is the starting point of ethics." But subjectivity is neither the end point nor the only point of ethics. Ethics begins with the recognition that we are not alone or the center of the universe. Ethics is always about self in the context of others. Ethics must be open to the voices of others. For feminist and ethicist Carol Gilligan, caring for others, being responsive to others, being ethical, begins with standing outside of the needs of self and talking and listening to others.

> Have the courage to use your own reason.
>
> **—A motto of the Enlightenment**

I'm convinced that reason can free us from our parochial obsession with self. Reason can force us out of the cocoon of self. It can force us beyond mundane issues and concerns. Reason requires us to experience life as a complex equation of others and not just a simple game of solitaire.

At its core, ethics is an attempt to apply logical reasoning to human decision making and behavior to come up with rules and procedures by which to direct and judge our interactions with others. Perhaps the most rigorous practitioner and high priest of this reason-based approach to ethics is Immanuel Kant (1724–1804). Kant took to heart Socrates' admonition that "we must all reason together," and he created an ethical system grounded on reason, impartiality, reciprocity, and logical duty to others.

Immanuel (Manelchen, or "Little Manny" to his mother) Kant was born and lived his entire life in Königsberg, East Prussia. The son of a tradesman, he was educated at the University of Königsberg and subsequently spent his entire 42-year career as a professor there. However, the breadth, scope, and effects of his writings and ideas far transcended the confines of his life in his provincial German hometown. Historian Frederick Copleston claims the influence and importance of Kant's writings and ideas made him simultaneously a product and a progenitor of the Enlightenment with its emphasis on rationality and the scientific method and its rejection of traditional social, religious, and political ideas and beliefs. Copleston and other scholars contend that Kant is to philosophy what William Shakespeare is to English literature. The work of both of these men of genius represent watersheds, defining moments, turning points in their respective disciplines.

Always uncomfortable with formal religion, but without denying the existence of God, Kant wanted to create an ethical system devoid of tradition and theology. He wanted an ethics based on reason and not on revelation and faith. He saw no need to evoke or to crank down God (Deus ex machina) to explain the

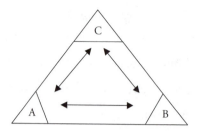

natural order. For Kant, there were rational reasons (prudence, practicality, the proximity of others, "the intrinsic worth and dignity of the individual") why individual A and individual B ought to show each other respect, civility, and due concern. For Kant, ethics is not a theological ménage à trois in which individual A and B are obligated to each other because they share the same first cause or creator, C.

Kant's Categorical Imperative

What Kant needed was a principle or set of principles that is known by reason before experience (a priori), self-evident and intuitively clear and correct, logically compelling and consistent, and universally true. Kant called this principle the "categorical imperative." (Although the categorical imperative is referred to in the singular, Kant offers us three formulations of this concept. For our purposes, we will limit ourselves to the first two versions of the definition.)

"Categorical" refers to a formula, a template, a methodological road map that we can apply to experience, and by which we recognize duty, or what we ought to do in a given situation. Kant did not believe that the moral life is merely the ability to achieve a good outcome or to be happy. The moral life is about doing what one ought to do, doing what is logically compelling, or doing what is logically necessary. For Kant, the categorical compels us to follow the dictates of reason and not our emotions or inclinations. Kant was convinced that as logical creatures we are obligated to recognize the validity of a proposition when we are no longer able to deny its logical claims. And we are obligated to act on that proposition when we recognize its validity.

THE FIRST CATEGORICAL

Kant's first formulation of the categorical imperative is this: "Act only according to that maxim (principle of action) by which your can, at the same time, will that it should become a universal law." Ronald M. Green, director of the Center for Ethics at Dartmouth College, has suggested that, in essence, what Kant achieved in the first formulation was to subject the Golden Rule to a committee of logicians so they can vote on it. In the pursuit of justice, fair treatment, and equality, Kant argues that logic requires us to ask, Given the particulars of a situation or problem, do I consider my action to be acceptable as a universal principle of conduct, even if, and especially if, it were used against me? Am I treating others the way I want to be treated? Am I treating others in the way I would want my loved ones to be treated? In other words, Kant asks us to hold up our solutions to a community of impartial moral agents and ask of them, "Is this rational? Is this acceptable, for one, for all?" Perhaps the Talmudic scholar Rabbi Hillel best captured the spirit of Kant's overall endeavor when in a debate he was challenged to explain all of ethics in a few sentences. His answer was an eloquent one: "What is hateful to you, do not do to another. This is the whole of the law, the rest is commentary."

THE SECOND CATEGORICAL

Kant's second formulation of the categorical imperative is this: "Act so that you treat humanity, whether in your person or in that of another, always as an end and never as a means only." Rational beings must be designated as persons, not things. They are ends in themselves, objects of intrinsic value and worth. As objects of respect, persons cannot be arbitrarily treated. We have a "direct duty," said Kant, never to use others or ourselves simply as a means to an end. Every person, says Kant, must endeavor, as far as possible, to further the well-being of others as well as one's own well-being.

As L. W. Beck, another commentator on Kant who has translated several of his works, observed,

> In our mechanized society we constantly run the danger of degrading man to an object rather than a subject, a thing rather than a person. Whenever we forget that our human employees differ radically from the machines which they operate, that our students are more than names on grade cards, that our wives are more than complex mechanisms with built-in attachments for performing household duties—whenever we destroy, degrade, or even ignore the unique values of human personality—we are guilty of the most profound of all moral sins. This is Kant's meaning in this formulation of the categorical imperative. It is also the essence of the moral teaching of Judaism and Christianity.

The bottom line of all of this is easier than it seems. Kant wanted to establish a rational benchmark for ethical behavior. He wanted to create a method of ethical decision making that was "free of the fortress of self," or, in the words of theologian Karen Armstrong, "outside the prism of self." He was convinced that the categorical imperative could serve as a template or a logical decision tree by which we could determine how to do the right thing, for the right reason, purposefully. An ethical action—a fair and a just action—is one that would be acceptable to anyone in a similar circumstance or situation. Individuals are ends in themselves and deserve respect and dignity. No person can or should be solely used as a pawn, a tool, for the betterment of another.

This book is not a book about Immanuel Kant, but it is about what Kant wanted to achieve. Ethics for Kant is about reason, not revelation, temperament, or emotions. Ethics is about logical rules that can be known and that apply to all. For Kant, ethics is primarily concerned with the *is/ought* distinction (a phrase that Kant did not use). That is, ethics is the study of *what we ought to do.* The *is* is what people do—the simple given, the factual. The *is* is the realm of science and general observation. The *ought* is the realm of ethics. The *ought* is evaluative: It asks of us not what we *could* do or what we would *like* to do, but rather what we logically *should* and *must* do.

Even though Kant wanted a system that was fixed, formal, and rational in nature, he was well aware that the moral enterprise is not like solving mathematical algorithms into which facts can be inserted and out of which results can be generated. He was well aware that our "moral disposition is in conflict" and that it is subject to temptation, desire, and distractions. And he lamented the fact that, to appropriate the twentieth-century terminology of British biologist Richard Dawkins, our "selfish genes" seek out and are both motivated by and tempted by much more than the merely rational. In fact, it can be argued that many of the reasons that motivate personal ethical behavior are totally self-serving and quiet pedestrian.

Can One Be Too Ethical?

PHILADELPHIA, Aug. 17—Having already given one kidney to a total stranger, Zee Kravinsky was sipping an orange-mango Snapple and, unprompted, making a case for giving away his other one.

"What if someone needed it who could produce more good than me?" Mr. Kravinsky said today in an interview. "What if I was a perfect match for a dying scientist who was the intellectual driving force behind a breakthrough cure for cancer or AIDS on the brink of unlocking the secrets of cell regeneration?"

—*New York Times*, **August 17, 2003**

This is not a self-help book on ethics. My intent is to be descriptive rather than prescriptive. I think Socrates was right when he suggested that you cannot answer ethical questions by simply appealing to what other people think. They may be wrong. Each of us must try to find an answer that we ourselves regard as correct. That is why this book is not full of answers. Nor does it contain a long ethical laundry list of do's and don'ts. My central focus is to examine some of the major reasons why it is so hard to be ethical, and why it is so hard to get free of the *emotional fortress of self*. In particular, I want to examine some of the social, cultural, physical, as well as psychological factors which feed and facilitate our self-absorption and discourages us from stepping outside of the narcissistic nexus of "me, myself, and I."

Some of the factors I want to examine are neither novel nor esoteric, but they individually and collectively have a profound effect on how we perceive the world, understand ourselves, and deal with others. Some of the factors I'm going to examine simply confuse us, wear us down, and/or exhaust us. Some frighten us, and some give us pleasure. All of them isolate us from the possibility of our better selves. They keep us from "listening to the needs of others" because we are too busy amusing ourselves, protecting ourselves, or insulating ourselves from ideas and realities that we do not want to deal with.

In the best of all possible worlds, it is never easy to do the right thing. It is always hard and often costly to extend ourselves to others. There is a reason we honor and praise those individuals who risk themselves in the service of others. Being a hero is a difficult thing to do, and being an ethical person is not always an easy thing to do. It entails energy, effort, and the willingness to step outside oneself.

The format and structure of this text is straightforward. The first three chapters are an attempt to unpack and define ethics as a theory, a discipline, a method, and as a general philosophical orientation toward life. The remaining eight chapters attempt to detail some, but by no means all, of the particular reasons why it is so difficult to be ethical, why it's so easy to be distracted from being ethical, and why it is so hard to get beyond the self.

1. Ethics Means *What?*

Those who are concerned with making the world more
healthy had but start with themselves. Finding the
center of strength within oneself is, in the long run,
the best contribution we can make to our fellow men.

—**William James**

He who knows not, and knows not that he knows not,
is a fool, shun him. But he who knows not, and knows
that he knows not, is a wise man, follow him!

—**Eastern proverb**

The most famous phrase in the history of the literature of philosophy is the Socratic dictum, "The unexamined life is not worth living." Perhaps the second-best-known philosophical nugget is René Descartes' *cogito, ergo sum*, "I think, therefore I am." It is at best a far distant second, however, and most often conjured up only while playing a game of Trivial Pursuit.

Less famously, *Chicago Tribune* essayist Terry Sullivan has said, "The examined life may be the ideal, but it's too hard to do. It requires too much of us. It requires us to be responsible to ourselves and others for the outcomes of our choices and actions. It requires us to be in charge of who we are." There are real truths to be mined from Socrates' and Sullivan's statements. And when closely examined side by side, these statements represent the Gordian knot or the central question of the entire ethical enterprise: What is the right thing to do? Or, more accurately, What ought I to do in regard to others?

The English philosopher and mathematician Alfred North Whitehead once said that "all of philosophy is but a footnote to Socrates/Plato." (Plato, of course, was a student of Socrates for 20 years and served as the chronicler and creator of the Socratic dialogues. As a teacher, Socrates would have perished long before he was ordered to drink hemlock, because he never published.) What Whitehead meant by this statement is that Socrates and Plato laid the groundwork for what Western philosophy was to become. Certainly, they were not the first philosophers; they were preceded by Thales, Anaximander, Pythagoras, Heraclitus, Parmenides, Zeno, and others. However, they were the first who left behind an entire corpus of work, and within this body of work we find most if not all the basic philosophical questions itemized and asked, even if they were not satisfactorily answered or resolved. For Whitehead, after Socrates and Plato, the rest of the history of philosophy has been an attempt to unpack, embellish, and formulate answers to the questions, topics, and problems that they raised.

Students of classical Greek history have long debated exactly where Socrates' thoughts and ideas left off and where Plato's began. Though there is no unanimity on the matter, most scholars agree that the dialogue *The Apology* is a reflection of Socrates' most fundamental philosophical beliefs. In *The Apology*, Socrates argues that the first principle and the first job of philosophy is to be able to grasp and understand the admonition of the oracle of Apollo at Delphi: *Gnothi seauton*, "Know thyself."

Socrates was "curiously unscientific" about his outlook on life. He said of himself that he had "nothing to do with physical speculations." Nor was he especially interested in one of Aristotle's primary preoccupations, metaphysics, which is the study of ultimate cause(s), purpose, and meaning of life. Rather than questioning the nature and structure of the cosmos, Socrates believed we would be better off questioning the cosmos within, our inner nature, our most intimate selves. For Socrates. the first question of philosophy is the self: Who am I? To answer the question of self, Socrates believed that we must ask questions that disturb, provoke, anger, and intimidate us. We must be willing to ask questions that shake and shift the ground under our feet. For Socrates, the question of self (Who am I?) precedes all other considerations, including the related question of self and others (What ought I to do with others?). As Socrates clearly stated in *The Republic*, "He who would rule the world must first rule himself."

In *The Apology*, Socrates argues that the first step toward wisdom is the discovery and acknowledgment of our own ignorance. He tells the story of his friend Chaerephon, who climbed up the slopes of Mount Parnassus and asked the oracle if there was a wiser man in all of Greece than Socrates of Athens. The priestess replied that there was no one wiser, and Socrates was shocked by the oracle's answer. "What can the god mean?" said Socrates. "I have no claim to wisdom, great or small." So Socrates decided this was a test, and he set out to find the wisest man in all of Greece. He talked to politicians, poets, skilled craftsmen, and many others thought to be wise. But all of them, said Socrates, although they appeared and pretended to be wise, were not. Moreover, he said, even when they did not know, they denied their ignorance and claimed wisdom. In the end, Socrates decided that the oracle was correct. He was the wisest man in all of Greece, or at least he was wise to this small extent: "I do not claim that I know what I do not know."

It is also in *The Apology* that Socrates declares for all Athenians to hear:

> I spent all my time going about trying to persuade you, young and old, to make your first and your chief concern not your bodies or your possessions, but for the highest welfare of your souls. . . . Wealth does not bring goodness, but goodness brings wealth and every other blessing, both to the individual and to the state. . . . Let no day pass without discussing goodness. . . . [This] is really the very best thing that a man can do, and . . . the life without this sort of examination is not worth living.

For Socrates and his modern successors in the "study of the mind" (*psuchē-logos*)—among whom we can identify Abraham Maslow, founder of "Third Force Psychology," and Sigmund Freud—the "examined life" is the result of self-awareness, self-reflection, and ultimately self-knowledge. It is only in coming to know ourselves, both our strengths and weaknesses, that we can begin to know and have sympathy, care, and concern for others. As Maslow so elegantly phrased it, "What we are blind and deaf to in ourselves, we are blind and deaf to in others." For Socrates, the art of living together in the *polis* (the city-state) and the science (by "science" the Greeks meant an activity that is studied rationally and systematically) of human behavior and conduct (in Greek *ethikā*, in Latin *mores, moralis*) start with self, but are lived out with others. For Socrates, the good life for self, the good life with others (an ethical life), is a life lived "according to what is reasonable" (*kata ton orthon logos*).

Ethics Is a Lived Activity

Many scholars believe that one of the central features of the Socratic dialogues is their lack of doctrinaire ideology. Socrates did not preach "a system." Rather Socrates was a teacher, and what he taught was not so much a philosophy as a philosophical system, a way of looking at the world, and a way of looking at self. The essence of his lesson plan was an elegant one: Let us all reason together. Let us talk with one another. For Socrates, clear thinking, clear reasoning, is a communal event, not a singular activity. Truth, as a way to achieve good behavior, is the result of thinking with and talking to others, a dialogue.

The dialectical method requires us to enter into conversation with others and to mutually debate and examine an idea or a subject matter. Theoretically, the dialogue proceeds from a less adequate definition, or from a consideration of particular examples, to a more general definition. (Metaphorically speaking, the dialectical method is the practice of holding a problem out at arm's length to better see it and gain a modicum of objectivity. In so examining the problem, alternative solutions are applied until the best possible one is hit upon.) Socratic scholar Gregory Vlastos described Socrates' method of inquiry as "among the greatest achievements of humanity." Why? Because, says Vlastos, it makes philosophical inquiry "a common human enterprise, open to every man." Instead of requiring allegiance to a specific philosophical viewpoint or analytical technique or specialized vocabulary, the Socratic method "calls for common sense and common speech." And this, says Vlastos, "is as it should be, for how a man should live is every man's business."

Christopher Phillips, author of the charming and insightful *Socrates Café*, argues that the Socratic method goes far beyond Vlastos' description. The method, says Phillips, does not merely call for common sense in our lives, but it also examines and critiques what common sense is in our lives. The method asks, Does the common sense (conventional wisdom) of our day offer us the greatest potential for self-understanding and ethical conduct? Or is the prevailing common sense in fact a roadblock to realizing this potential? According to Phillips, the Socratic method forces people to confront their own dogmatism by asking such basic questions as, What does this mean? What speaks for and against it? Are there other ways of considering the issue that are even more plausible and tenable? In compelling us to explore alternative perspectives, says Phillips, the method forces us to think outside the box and be open to the opinions of others.

For Socrates, we are "questioning beings," and it is only through questioning life and others that we begin to have a better understanding of self. In fact, he suggests that the process of questioning is more important than the answers arrived at. When Socrates said, "The unexamined life is not worth living," what is implied is that in examining life, in questioning life, we may not come up with an answer. Or we may simply generate a series of new questions, or worse yet, arrive at an answer that we cannot or will not accept. Nevertheless, Socrates seemed convinced that the greater error, the bigger danger, lies with not asking any questions at all. In asking questions we say and assert something about ourselves. In asking, we have hope, but we also recognize that there are no guarantees. And, in asking, we reveal a great deal about who we are and who we would like to be.

In *The Apology*, with his very life in the balance, Socrates retains his conviction that the greatest danger of all is to dispense with questioning and examining our lives.

As long as I breathe and have the strength to go on, I won't quit
philosophizing. I won't quit exhorting you and whomever I happen
to meet, in my customary way: Esteemed friend, citizen of Athens,
the greatest city in the world, so outstanding in both intelligence and
power, aren't you ashamed to care so much to make all the money you
can, and to advance your reputation and prestige—while for truth and
wisdom and the improvement of your soul you have no care or worry?

For Socrates, philosophy was a way of life, a way of approach-
ing and seeing the world, a way of thinking. In the end, the
Socratic method is as much about the process as the product, as
much about the journey as the destination. In fact, I think it is
fair to say that what Socrates left us was not a series of answers,
but, rather, a process and a purposeful way of thinking. In the
words of Ludwig W. Wittgenstein, "Philosophy is not (just) a
theory but an activity."

Like Socrates' general approach to philosophy, ethics is best
understood as a general attitude and orientation toward life. In
other words, ethics is as much a methodology and an activity as it
is a theory. It is a way of looking at the world, a way of thinking.
It is not just a fixed body of knowledge. It is not just a doctrine
with specific rules. It is not just a series of answers. Ethics is
something we live out with others. And in this "living out" we
are constantly asking ourselves three fundamental questions:
Who am I? What do I owe others? What ought I to do?

It is of course impossible not to recognize the brute fact
that since Socrates' time, ethics has become, to say the least, a
growth industry. As a formal discipline there are many different

schools of thought (theories) regarding the ethical enterprise. These theories range from Aristotle's virtue ethics to Thomas Hobbes' social contract theory of justice, Immanuel Kant's logic of duty, Jeremy Bentham's and J. S. Mill's utilitarianism/consequentialism, Thomas Aquinas' natural law theory, Ayn Rand's virtue of selfishness, and Jean-Paul Sartre's radical existentialism. Although these ethical theories, and a long list of others, offer radically divergent approaches and perspectives on what constitutes an ethically acceptable act, they are all equally committed to answering the same philosophical question: How should we live together?

Psychologist and pundit Robert R. Provine has suggested that although ethics is a laudable endeavor, he's not at all sure that Socrates' dialectical method is the best way to approach the issue. "Philosophy," he says, "is to science what alcohol is to sex: It may stir the imagination, fire the passions, and get the process underway, but the act and implementation may be flawed, and the end result may come up short." Provine believes that many philosophers fail because they have "an overly optimistic estimate of the power of naked reason and a dependence on anecdotal evidence." Well, maybe we do! No, in fact, we definitely do! But what alternative do we have? Not all things regarding the mind and the heart are susceptible to measurement and quantification. Not every problem of human life and relationships can be clinically diagnosed and remedied by following a recommended pharmacological protocol. In resolving most ethical problems, says philosophical practitioner Lou Marinoff, what we need is Plato, not Prozac.

Ethics begins with the recognition that we are not alone or the center of the universe. We are not herd animals, but we are communal creatures. We are dependent on one another. We are born by others, live with the help of others, and function, survive, and thrive only with the assistance of others. We are collective by nature and necessity. For Jean-Paul Sartre, like it or not, we are by definition moral creatures because we are "condemned" by the fact of our collective existence to continually make choices about what we ought to do in regard to others. Ethics is, I think, primarily a communal collective enterprise, not a solitary one. It is the study of our web of reciprocal relationships with others. When Robinson Crusoe found himself marooned and alone on a tiny Pacific atoll, all things were possible. But when Friday came along and they discovered pirates burying treasure and each other on the beach, Crusoe was then involved in a universe of others, an ethical universe. As a communal exercise, ethics is the attempt to work out the rights and obligations we have and share with others. What is mine? What do I owe you? An act is not wrong (unethical) simply because it advances the well-being of an individual, but an act is wrong if it is unfair and inconsiderate in regard to the rights and just claims of others.

All ethical judgments are in some sense a "values versus values" or "rights versus rights" confrontation. Unfortunately, the question of what we ought to do in relation to the values and rights of others cannot be reduced to the analogue of a simple litmus test. In fact, I believe that all of ethics is based on what William James called the "will to believe." That is, we choose to believe, despite the ideas, arguments, and reasoning to the contrary, that individuals possess certain basic rights that cannot and should not be willfully disregarded or overridden by others. In "choosing to believe," said James, we establish this belief as a factual baseline of our thought process for all considerations in regard to others. Without this "reasoned choice," says James, the enterprise loses its "vitality" in human interactions.

According to Harvard philosopher John Rawls, given the presence of others and that we need others, ethics is elementally the pursuit of justice, fair play, and equity. For Rawls, the study of ethics has to do with developing standards for judging the conduct of one party whose behavior affects another. Minimally, "good behavior" intends no harm and respects the rights of all affected, and "bad behavior" willfully or negligently tramples on the rights and interests of others. Ethics, then, tries to find a way to protect one person's individual rights and needs against and alongside the rights and needs of others. Of course, the paradox and central tension of ethics lies in the fact that although we are by nature communal and in need of others, we are by disposition more or less egocentric and self-serving.

John Dewey has argued that at the pre-critical, pre-rational, pre-autonomous stage of our lives, morality is experienced as culturally defined rules that are external to us and are imposed or

Ethics

- Ethics is the pursuit of:
  - Justice
  - Fairness/Fair Play
  - Equal Treatment
  - Equitable Treatment
- Ethics is an attempt to work out the rights and obligations we have and share with others. (What is mine? And what do I owe you?)
- Ethics tries to resolve the fundamental paradox of human experience:
  - We are all by disposition (more/less) egocentric or self-centered.
  - We are all by nature collective, or in need of others.
- Ethics is an attempt to balance our ego needs against and along with the ego needs of others.
- Ethics is the attempt to be objective/impartial with others, even when personal interests are at stake.

inculcated as habits. But real ethical thinking, said Dewey, begins at the evaluative period of our lives, when as independent agents we freely decide to accept, embrace, modify, or deny these rules. Dewey maintained that every serious ethical system rejects the notion that one's standard of conduct should simply and uncritically be an

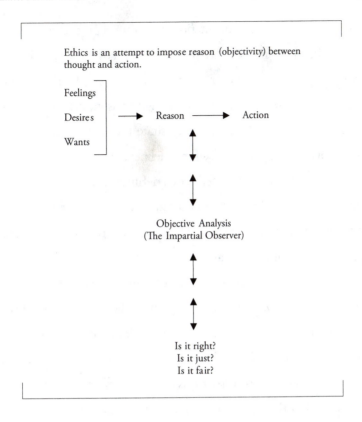

Ethics is an attempt to impose reason (objectivity) between thought and action.

acceptance of the rules of the culture we happen to live in. Even if it is the case that custom, habit, convention, public opinion, or law are correct in their mandates, to embrace them without critical reflection does not constitute a complete and formal ethical act and might be better labeled "ethical happenstance" or "ethics by virtue of circumstantial accident." For Dewey, ethics is essentially "reflective conduct," and he believed that the distinction between custom and reflective morality is clearly marked. The former places the standard and rules of conduct solely on habit, the latter appeals to reason and choice. The distinction is as important as it is definite, for it shifts the center of gravity in morality. For Dewey, ethics is a two-part process. It is never enough simply to do the right thing. We must do the right thing for the right reason, purposefully. In other words, true ethical acts necessitate the unity of theory and action or the integration of self in a deliberately chosen act.

Perhaps the two most felicitous definitions of ethics I've ever come across are those of philosopher Ed Freeman and theologian Frank Griswald. "Ethics is how we treat people face to face, person to person, day in and day out over a prolonged period of time" (Freeman). "Ethics is about the rules we choose to live by once we decide we want to live together" (Griswald). What both of these definitions emphasize is that ethics is an ongoing task, a continual struggle. Both these definitions emphasize that ethics does exist as a *theory* but that it is only truly *alive* when practiced face to face. Ethics is something we do. It is an option, a choice. It is something that we make, create, build, maintain, and sustain with our decision making and our actions. Sounds simple, but it isn't! If it were simple, we could franchise it.

Ethics R' Us

- Four philosophers—no waiting
- All major brands of ethics, all the time
- Locations nationwide
- Franchises currently available

Ethics is difficult because it requires us to be concerned about the rights and well-being of others. It requires us to stop thinking of ourselves as the center of the universe. It requires us to transcend our narrow self-interest and to be just, rational, and objective. It requires us to take a stance, make a decision. Even when we try to avoid making a decision, we often can't. Most moral problems do not allow us the luxury of neutrality. In the words of Harvey Cox, "Not to decide, is to decide." But perhaps the ultimate reason ethics is so difficult for us is because it requires us to do something we either "cannot" or do not want to do—*be our very best selves in regard to others.*

Why Do the Right Thing?

Ultimately all of ethics revolves around the resolution of one basic question: Why should anyone do what is right when doing so is not to that person's advantage? Clearly it is not always personally advantageous to do the right thing. In fact, people are credited with high moral worth or are called heroes for doing what is right when this is contrary to their own best interest. The point is, if a person wants to be shown that it is always to her personal advantage to act morally—and that her life will invariably be better, or at least will not made worse—if she adopts the moral way of life, this demand will not be met. It must be admitted that anyone who takes the moral road may be called upon to make serious personal sacrifices and, hence, may not have as good a life at the material and practical levels as she would otherwise have had.

Perhaps the only response to this question is a negative one. It was Aristotle who fathered the notion that at the foundation of morals lies the principle that if morality is to be argued about at all, then the onus of justification lies upon those who propose to deny it.

Trooper's Dilemma

An auto mechanic was called early one morning to the scene of a wreck on a state highway. Arriving at the isolated, wooded spot, he could see immediately what had happened; a large flatbed truck had gone off the highway and hit a tree head-on. On impact, its load of steel had torn loose and slid forward through the back of the cab, pinning the driver helplessly inside. The cab was on fire, in danger of exploding at any minute.

As he arrived, so did a state police car. And as the trooper ran to the open cab window, the mechanic could hear the driver inside screaming, "Shoot me! Shoot me!" It was obvious that the trooper could not lift off the load of steel and free the driver. So, with the flames growing in intensity, the trooper slowly removed his service revolver from his holster. Then he paused and reconsidered. Q: What would you do? (See below for what the trooper actually did.)

I think that the entire history of ethical thought in the Western tradition can be traced back to the Socratic dictum that "the unexamined life is not worth living." In some sense, every ethical system since Socrates has been an attempt to live the examined life. However, no ethical system can sustain prolonged, ruthless analysis. And because no system of thought can guarantee ethical truth, perhaps the only thing that really matters is the individual's attempt and commitment to the process of trying to arrive at ethical truths. Although "perennial truths" may not exist, there are certain "perennial questions" that are endemic to the human condition, questions that each succeeding generation must answer for itself: Who am I? Why am I? What is the meaning of life? What do I owe others? Thomas Aquinas once said that there were three things necessary for the ethical life: (1) to know what we ought to believe, (2) to know what we ought to desire, and (3) to know what we ought to do.

Given all of this, I believe ethics is the art, not a science, of living well and of knowing what one ought or ought not do. Its primary focus of attention is centered on the question, What does it mean to be human, within the limits of the world and the context of others? Ethics is the endeavor to achieve the good life on both the individual and social levels. As an art, the art of living, it is something acquired, done, or lived out. It is not innate or merely given. Like learning to drive a car or being a doctor or a lawyer, it is an acquired technique that one must consciously master. It is a skill that one must learn before one can do it well, or perhaps do it at all.

Answer (Trooper's Dilemma)

The trooper "paused, reconsidered, and slid the revolver back into his holster. And then, amid the driver's screams he removed it a second time, paused, and put it back once again.

It was at that point in this agonized struggle that the mechanic saw the officer do a remarkable thing. Running back to the cruiser, he grabbed a small carbon tetrachloride fire extinguisher. It was large enough to spray in the driver's face and put him to sleep, which is what he did.

Shortly afterward, the cab exploded."

2. Narcissism: Me, Myself, and I

First comes eating, then comes morality.

—**Bertolt Brecht**

Perhaps the single overarching problem regarding all forms of ethical behavior and conduct is getting free of the shadow of self, that is, being impartial and overcoming our natural tendency to be self-absorbed in our interactions with others. The central paradox of communal existence lies in the tension that exists between our essential need for others and our hard-core egocentrism and selfishness. Empathy, concern for others, may be instinctive in our regard for babies and puppies, but in regard to all others, it is often an acquired, learned, and sometimes imposed characteristic or tendency. Fundamental to the ethical enterprise is a question that too many of us find difficult to answer: Why is it so hard to see past the needs and wants of self?

In Greek mythology, the legend of Narcissus is told in a number of slightly different ways, but all of the versions end with the same moral message. As a child and a young man, Narcissus was so beautiful that many lovers, men and women alike, courted him, but he refused them all. (Even the nymph Echo fell in love with him. The grieving Echo pined away until she was only a voice in the mountains, uttering forever the last syllable of any word that she heard.) One erstwhile lover rejected by Narcissus prayed to Nemesis (the personification of retribution), who condemned Narcissus to contemplate his own beauty reflected in a pool of water on Mount Helicon. Maddened by the sight of his own face, Narcissus could not tear himself away from the pool. Hour after hour, day after day, Narcissus hung over the pool's edge. He had no care for food or drink; he only gazed at the reflection he loved.

> "Why, beautiful being [Narcissus says to his own reflection],
> do you shun me? Surely, my face is not one to repel you.
> The nymphs love me, and you yourself look not indifferent
> upon me. When I stretch forth my arms you do the same;
> and you smile upon me and answer my beckonings with the
> like. . . . Stay, I entreat you! Let me at least gaze upon you, if
> I may not touch you."

Hour after hour, day after day, Narcissus hung over the pool's edge. He had no care for food or drink; he only gazed at the reflection he loved. Now it was Narcissus' time for heartsick grief. "Now I know," he wept, "what others have suffered from me, for I burn with love of another self." Crying in vain for the object of his adoration, his heart finally ceased to throb, and he lay dead on the shore. The story ends with the gods themselves taking pity on so fair a corpse and transforming his body into a new and lovely flower they called Narcissus.

Sigmund Freud sometimes used the term "narcissism" in the colloquial sense of being self-absorbed, self-centered. But at other times, he used it to denote any of an array of psychiatric stages and disorders: a sexual perversion in which individuals use their own bodies or body parts as objects of self-arousal; a transitional characteristic in a specific developmental phase, such as the phallic or genital stages; and a condition of chronic personality disorder.

According to the *Synopsis of Psychiatry*, persons with narcissistic personality disorder are characterized by a heightened sense of self-importance and grandiose feelings that they are unique in some way. They consider themselves special people and expect special treatment. They always want their own way and are frequently ambitious, desiring fame and fortune. Their relationships with others are fragile and limited. They are unable to show empathy, and they feign sympathy for others only to achieve their own selfish ends. Interpersonal exploitation is commonplace.

The narcissistic personality is readily identifiable. This is the person who:

- is self-absorbed
- exaggerates his/her own worth
- shows no empathy
- feels entitled
- seeks attention
- can't take criticism
- loves flattery
- expects special treatment
- tries to control God
- exempts himself or herself from rules
- manipulates others
- lacks gratitude

The term "narcissism" or "narcissistic type" is not often used in philosophical circles, but I think it should be. The concept of narcissism neatly encapsulates the dark side of why it is so hard to get free of the shadow of self.

There are, however, some benign and even critically beneficial reasons why it is so hard to get free of our absorption in self. Evolutionary psychologist Robert Wright has argued that we are indeed "the moral animal" because we are social creatures who are rational and evaluative by nature. But before our ancestors were human, before they were primates, before they were mammals—way, way back through the evolution of our brain—there is a reptilian core. For Wright, the human brain is a "triune" brain, and its three basic parts recapitulate our evolution. Biologically speaking, says Wright, though our "neomammalian brain" made us human by giving us abstract reasoning and language, it is the instinctive behaviors of our reptilian and mammalian brains that kept us alive long enough to become humans.

Simple survival requires self-absorption. Being self-centered, overly cautious, hypersensitive, and/or alternatively aggressively defensive or defensively aggressive toward all external stimuli are qualities that are life enhancing, not examples of egocentrism. At the biological level, from both an individual and species point of view, being preoccupied, excessively self-absorbed, and interpersonally exploitive are virtues and not a vice. These are survival mechanisms, not adverse personality traits. Virtually all animals must be keenly aware of their surroundings, and any kind of change can trigger patterns of flight or fight. Being narcissistic, for the reptilian, paleomammalian, and, yes, neo-mammalian brains, is a biologically beneficial trait and part and parcel of our "hardwiring."

> Man is an animal with primary instincts of survival. Consequently, his ingenuity has developed first and his soul afterwards. Thus the progress of science is far ahead of man's ethical behavior.
>
> **—Charlie Chaplin**

Unfortunately, at the social level, the neomammalian brain has converted a biological virtue into a psychological and ethical vice. A narcissistic individual's entire sense of self is devoted to the pursuit of personal pleasure and self-gratification with little or no concern for the wants and needs of others. Narcissists are not necessarily vain in the cosmetic sense of clothing, style, or trends, but, cosmologically speaking, the world begins and revolves around them. Narcissists create for themselves a self-defined, self-contained, self-serving worldview, which rationalizes anything done on their behalf and which does not require justification on any grounds outside themselves.

In *The Culture of Narcissism*, historian Christopher Lasch argues that to live for the moment, to live for yourself, and not for your contemporaries, predecessors, or posterity is America's prevailing ethical leitmotif. Narcissists feel free to abandon their social roles as parent, neighbor, or citizen for the higher purpose and goal of self-fulfillment and self-gratification. Lasch sees in the nineteenth-century ideal of "rugged individualism" an outwardly oriented worldview that saw the world as a "wilderness to be shaped and won with and for others." In contrast, contemporary individualism, says Lasch, is totally self-absorbed, and "the world is a mirror." People busy themselves with efforts to improve what they see in the mirror:

Americans have retreated to purely personal preoccupations. Having no hope of improving their lives in any of the ways that matter, people have convinced themselves that what matters is psychic self-improvement: getting in touch with their feelings, eating health food, taking lessons in ballet or belly-dancing, immersing themselves in the wisdom of the East, jogging, learning how to relate, overcoming the fear of pleasure.

Techniques of Self-Absorption

The techniques and touchstones of narcissistic personality types are extensive, often complicated and convoluted, and are most often dependent on the situation, circumstance, as well as the particular personalities and issues involved. The following is but a short list of what I take to be some of the key methods and behaviors that narcissistic personality types implement in order to insulate and isolate themselves from themselves and others and, thereby stay within the shadow of self.

INSTANT GRATIFICATION

One of the fundamental reasons a lot of us, narcissistic types and otherwise, are unable to be overly concerned with ethical considerations is our tendency to overvalue present gratification and to undervalue future possible benefits and goods. The ability to defer gratification is one of the best measurements of emotional and ethical maturity. The problem is that people who live in the immediate moment tend to dismiss the past because it is no more, and they tend to give no thought to the future because it has not yet arrived. Such a position is, I believe, impoverishing because it lacks perspective. Ethically speaking, reality is the moment, but only as it comes from the past and leads us into the future. All three dimensions must be considered in order to develop a consistent and ethically attuned character. The same obsession with the present that has motivated U.S. citizens in the past few years to spend 98 percent of everything they earn—making for the lowest savings rate ever—also prevents them from developing a fullness of perspective that is essential to the moral life. Narcissistic types do not merely live in the moment; they are trapped in the moment and captives of its limitations.

THE LACK OF MORAL IMAGINATION

If ethics is an attempt to stir us beyond the numbness of self, then ethical decision making requires us to look beyond the immediate moment and beyond personal needs, desires, and wants in order to *imagine* the possible consequences of our decisions and behavior on self and others. In its most elemental sense, moral imagination is about picturing various outcomes in our interactions with others. In some sense, moral imagination is a dramatic virtual rehearsal that allows us to examine and appraise different courses of action in order to determine the morally best thing to do. The capacity for empathy is crucial to moral imagination. As Adam Smith wrote, "As we have no immediate experience of what other men feel, we can form no idea of the manner in which they are affected, but by conceiving what we ourselves should feel in the situation."

According to philosopher Patricia H. Werhane, a failure of this capacity—an inability to imagine and to be sympathetic to the needs, passions, and interests of others—causes moral ineptitude more frequently than do a lack of logic or ignorance of moral principles. Werhane writes that to sympathize is to place myself in another's situation, "not because of how that situation might affect me, but rather as if I were that person in that situation." Being imaginative, using "moral imagination," allows us to be self-reflective and to step back from our situation so as to see it from another point of view. In taking such a perspective, says Werhane, a person tries to look at the world or herself from a more dispassionate perspective or from the point of view of a dispassionate, reasonable person who is not wholly absorbed with self. Werhane calls this transpositional perspective "a disengaged view from somewhere," and within it a number of questions become obligatory: (1) What would a reasonable person judge is the right thing to do? (2) Could one defend this decision publicly? (3) What kind of precedent does this decision set? Would one want it repeated or made into law? (4) Is this decision or action necessary? (5) Is this the least worse option?

What Werhane is suggesting is that one must, in making an ethical decision, determine the answers to some crucial questions: What's at stake? What are the issues? Who else is involved? And what are the alternatives? Moral imagination allows us the possibility of addressing these questions from a perspective that is both inside and outside the box, a perspective that focuses on self and others.

Minimal Preconditions for Ethics

1. Belief that life is precious and/or sacred.
2. Belief that no individual self is the center of or the primary purpose of the universe.
3. Belief that all individuals have and share certain basic rights.
4. Belief that all individuals have and share certain basic obligations, responsibilities, and duties.

—**Simon Blackburn**

CALLOUSNESS, CARELESSNESS, AND HABIT

In 1963, Hannah Arendt coined a phrase in her book on the trial of Adolph Eichmann, *Eichmann in Jerusalem*, that remains rife with ethical implications. The phrase was "the banality of evil," and by it she meant the commonness and unspectacular nature of evil and evildoers. She had expected Eichmann to be powerful, vile, vicious, nonrepentant—in short, the devil incarnate. Instead he was a small, balding man who liked to read and who complained to his jailers about his nightly bouts of constipation and how the snobbish politics of the SS kept him from being promoted to full colonel. To Arendt's horror, both as a Jew and a philosopher, Eichmann was not writ large. He was not a monster. He was, rather, a self-involved, boring little clerk. A clerk, said Arendt, who carried out every order given to him, including transporting millions of Jews to their deaths in concentration camps. "Eichmann did not hate Jews, and that made it worse, to have no feelings," Arendt wrote. "To make Eichmann appear a monster renders him less dangerous than he was. If you kill a monster you can go to bed and sleep, for there aren't many of them. But if Eichmann was normality, then this is a far more dangerous situation."

Arendt pointed out that for Eichmann, everything beyond his orders, his own well- being, and his own twisted sense of duty and honor was irrelevant. Putting aside the issues of genocide and genuine evil, the same modus operandi compels narcissistic personality types. Just as Eichmann is the embodiment of the "banality of evil," the narcissist's lifestyle exemplifies "the irrelevance of others." Narcissistic types are not necessarily cruel or mean or evil, but they are serenely unconcerned or indifferent to others. They are hardened, thickened, calloused to the plight or needs of others. A colleague once pointed out to me, "It's not so much that self-absorbed, narcissistic types are consciously unethical. Rather, they are thoughtless and, in reality, unconscious of others. In fact, they may be genuinely amoral [without moral concern] in regard to others." In time, of course, callousness, carelessness, and self-absorbed indifference progress from simple behavior traits to habits, and eventually they become a way of life that influences if not totally dictates our moral worldview and the choices we make regarding others.

There is unfortunately an even darker side to the habit of callousness and carelessness in regard to others. It is what Nobel Prize winner Konrad Lorenz called pseudo-speciation. From the behavioral point of view, pseudo-speciation is a variation of what sociologists have traditionally referred to as ethnocentrism and its vicious half-brother, racial prejudice. Ethnocentrism, the idea that what is humane and good is defined by the values of one's own group, seems to be a common human experience. As such, ethnocentrism contributes to hostile intergroup images by accentuating the differences between a person's values and habits and those of people who belong to other groups. The beliefs and habits of other people are viewed as discrepant, esoteric, and incomprehensible. Behaviorally, ethnocentrism involves the rejection of members of other groups simply because they are outsiders.

In extreme situations, war for example, nothing is easier than for the human spirit to neglect to recognize in others the same conditions and characteristics that define and specify one's own humanity. Conflict tends to accentuate the differences between groups. Pseudo-speciation serves the psychological function of image replacement; through its use, human beings become others, objects, or *untermenschen* (German for subhumans). It is, as psychoanalyst Erik Erikson put it, "a process by which an 'enemy' traditionally is deprived of membership in the human race proper, thus solving the problem of guilt, if only on the surface."

At the individual level, pseudo-speciation is nothing more than the narcissistic self-proclamation that my actions, my thoughts, my standards, and my life are correct and should be emulated by all. Lorenz has stated that, at the social/cultural level, pseudo-speciation allows us to consider members of groups other than our own as not fully human (a pseudo-species) or at least to regard them as inferior, crude, and contemptuous rivals not worthy of common decency. Pseudo-speciation allows us to denude others of their humanity and individuality so that we do not kill men but abstract caricatures: Nazis, commies, capitalistic dogs, redskins, Japs, gooks. Psychoanalyst Erich Fromm said that in pseudo-speciation, the aggressor cuts the other person off emotionally and freezes him in an un-empathetic state. The other ceases to be experienced as a human and becomes a thing. Under these circumstances, there are no inhibitions against even the most severe forms of destructiveness. Moreover, said Fromm, there is good clinical evidence for the assumption that most destructive violence occurs in conjunction with momentary or chronic emotional withdrawal and general indifference to the plight of others.

Not surprisingly, this destruction of the humanness of an opponent comes to its peak when soldiers face enemies of different ethnic features. The Vietnam War is a prime example of this point. Being flown 10,000 miles from home to a strange, exotic land of dense jungles and tropical heat, confronted by a completely alien culture, abject poverty, and political corruption, then forced to engage in a civil war primarily fought with guerrilla tactics naturally exacerbated the U.S. soldiers' sense of uneasiness. This mixture of mystery, fear, death, suffering, and confusion led to the need for *untermenschen*, for gooks. This transformation of men into gooks justified the victimization of the Vietnamese and allowed for the application of a modified version of the U.S. frontier's resolution of the "Indian problem": "The only good gook is a dead gook!" According to psychiatrist Robert J. Lifton, the "gook syndrome" became an essential part of the collective psychological adaptation of Americans to the inverse moral universe of Vietnam. Avoiding the gook syndrome while in Vietnam was almost impossible. To rebel against it was to risk severe psychic and physical repercussions and possibly to endanger one's own life and the lives of others. As one former infantry sergeant made clear in telling of his own conflicts with the gook syndrome,

> I really felt sick at myself for not . . . confronting my men . . . and yet [I knew] . . . it wouldn't make any difference. I could . . . punish my troops when I caught them [calling the Vietnamese gooks or brutalizing them], and yet the whole military establishment was contrary to what I was doing. . . . The colonels called them Gooks, the captains called them Gooks, the staff all called them Gooks. . . . The men took their cue from that, and they considered me some kind of weird freak. . . . What could I do? . . . So I just had to sort of find a deadspace and put it all there.

Sadly, said Lifton, maintaining that "deadspace," creating that psychic numbing, meant ceasing to feel the humanity of the Vietnamese. And in some way, it also meant colluding in their victimization.

Pseudo-Speciation—SS Mission Statement

We must be honest, decent, loyal, and comradely to members of our own blood, and to nobody else. What happens to the Russians, what happens to the Czechs, is a matter of total indifference to me. What there is among the nations in the way of good blood of our kind, we will take for ourselves—if necessary, by kidnapping their children and raising them among us. Whether the other nations live in prosperity or croak from hunger interests me only insofar as we need them for slaves for our culture; otherwise, it does not interest me. Whether 10,000 Russian females drop from exhaustion while building an anti-tank ditch interests me only insofar as the anti-tank ditch gets finished for Germany's sake. We shall never be brutal and heartless where it is not necessary—obviously not. We Germans, the only people in the world who have a decent attitude toward animals, will also take a decent attitude toward these human animals. But it is a crime against our own blood to worry about them and to give them ideals that will make it still harder for our sons and grandsons to cope with them. . . . Our concern, our duty, is to our own people and our blood. . . . Toward anything else we can be indifferent. . . . I wish the SS to take this attitude in confronting the problem of all alien, non-Germanic peoples, especially the Russians. All else is just soap bubbles.

—Heinrich Himmler, October 2, 1943

ARRESTED DEVELOPMENT

There is yet another way to try to explain, if not justify, our collective preoccupation with "me, myself, and I." Let's refer to it as *incomplete ethical development* or *arrested ethical development*. The research and empirical investigations of psychologist and philosopher Lawrence Kohlberg convinced him that as we mature cognitively, our thinking about ethics expands and matures as well, and we acquire an increasingly more rational and objective ethical outlook that is rooted in abstract moral principles and not on personal needs, taste, and preference. Putting aside for now the debate that "ethical styles," "ethical choices," and "ethical stages" may be gender specific and that Kohlberg studied only male subjects, Kohlberg's larger point was that all moral development follows a universal and irreversible sequence. As individuals progress from stage to stage, they become more rational, more rule and duty bound, more empathetic to the rights and needs of others, and they develop a more ideal universal perspective on human rights, justice, and reciprocity.

Kohlberg's Stages of Moral Development

Preconventional Level: "Right and wrong are based on our notion of pleasure and pain."

Stage 1:   *The Punishment and Obedience Orientation*: Good is what the person with power says is good. Doing good avoids punishment.

Stage 2:   *The Instrumental Relativism Orientation*: Right and wrong are about need, efficiency, and—"You scratch my back, I'll scratch yours."

Conventional Level: "Right and wrong are based on expectations of family, friends, and the rules of society."

Stage 3: *Good Boy—Nice Girl Orientation*: We act to gain approval.

Stage 4: *Law and Order Orientation*: We act to please authority, maintain the status quo.

Postconventional Level: "An objective, rational understanding of the reasoning behind moral rules."

Stage 5: *The Social-Contract Legalistic Orientation*: Something is right and fair only if it impartially respects the basic rights of all involved and advances the common good.

Stage 6: *The Universal Ethical Principal Orientation*: Justice and fairness must be accorded to everyone because of the fundamental equality and dignity of all human beings.

—**Thomas I. White**

According to commentator Thomas I. White, Kohlberg argues that in the process of moral development, we go from "preconventional" to "conventional" and then to "postconventional" morality. "Preconventional" morality defines good in terms of raw power and self-interest. "Conventional" morality recognizes the interest of others and the legitimacy of authority and law. "Postconventional" morality emphasizes autonomous ethical thinking, and ultimately focuses on principles of justice. As Kohlberg succinctly explains it,

In the preconventional and conventional levels, moral content or value is largely accidental or culture-bound. Anything from "honesty" to "courage in battle" can be the central value. But in the higher postconventional levels, Socrates, Lincoln, Thoreau, and Martin Luther King Jr. tend to speak without a confusion of tongues, as it were. This is because the ideal principles of any social structure are basically alike, if only because there simply aren't that many principles which are articulate, comprehensive and integrated enough to be satisfying to the human intellect. And most of these principles have gone by the name of justice.

Although Kohlberg claims that all normal development begins for everyone in stage 1 and proceeds sequentially, there are no guarantees that everyone makes it to stage 6. As a friend of mine put it, "I know a lot of CEOs and Ph.D. types with lots of degrees, lots of money, lots of great stuff going on in their lives. But when it comes to dealing with others, they're like kids, caught in stages 1, 2, and maybe 3. They know how to play the game. Nice words, Good manners. But in fact, they're only out to take care of numero uno, and the only time they do the right thing is because it's in their own best interest. It all comes down to a case of arrested development."

I think my friend is right. And I think that Niccolò Machiavelli would agree with him, too. For Machiavelli, the primary imperative of the Prince is to hold on to power and live long enough to enjoy it. To achieve this end, said Machiavelli, the Prince must be willing to do anything. The Prince must be strong and resolute, and he must at times be cruel. But all the while he is doing these things, he must use his best manners, evoke the highest standards, and portray himself as the defender of the people's rights and the champion of justice (stages 5, 6). In fact, of course, the Prince's motivation is much simpler: "I want what I want, when I want it! And I don't want to be punished for doing it" (stages 1, 2). Although Machiavelli would never have used the term, the Prince must, if he is to survive, be a highly practiced and successful "narcissist" who is, by choice and character, unable and unwilling to get free of the shadow of self.

3. Character, Integrity, and Conscience

One's bearing [character] shapes one's fate.

—**Heraclitus**

Winston Churchill reportedly once said of a political opponent, "Deep down, there's a lot less there than meets the eye." He was, of course, referring to the person's character or lack thereof. And it is just this phenomenon, the absence of character or, to be more precise, the presence of flawed character that goes a long way toward explaining the difficulty that so many people have in figuring out what they ought to do in an ethical situation. Aristotle suggested, as did British philosopher G. E. M. Anscombe and many others, that to do ethics properly you must start with what a person needs and must have in order to flourish and live well with others: character. For Aristotle, the ethical life is grounded on the development and expression of character.

A detailed taxonomy of the philosophical literature on the role and function of character would require a number of books. Even a cursory analysis of the topic is a daunting task. And yet, colloquially speaking, we all are more or less aware of what the term generally means. Social scientist James Q. Wilson has argued that when we describe people we admire or like, we rarely define them by any one trait. Rather, we make judgments about others based on a set of traits, a character. By character, said Wilson, we mean two things: (1) a distinctive combination of personal qualities by which someone is known, that is, a personality, and (2) a distinctive combination of moral strengths, moral values, and integrity.

The root of the word "character" is the Greek word for etching or engraving. *Charaktêr* was originally used to signify the marks impressed upon a coin. As applied to human beings, *charaktêr* refers to the enduring marks or etched-in factors that have been impressed on a person's mind, her *psyche*, which include her inborn talents as well as learned and acquired traits gleaned from education and experience. These engravings set individuals apart, define them, and motivate behavior.

Although much of character is imposed on us, engraved on us by the socioeconomic environment, the vagaries of time and place, and the biological (genetic) and behavioral influences of our parents, character is also about what a person chooses to hold dear, chooses to value, and chooses to believe in. To paraphrase the words of Eleanor Roosevelt, if you want to know what a person values, check their checkbooks. If you want to know about a person's character, check their values. And if you want to know a person's ethics, check their character.

In *Character: America's Search for Leadership*, Gail Sheehy argues that character is the most crucial and most elusive element of leadership. In regard to leadership, says Sheehy, character is fundamental and prophetic. The issues of leadership, says Sheehy, "are today and will change in time. Character is what was yesterday and will be tomorrow." Character establishes both our day-to-day demeanor and our destiny. Therefore, it is essential to examine the character of those who desire to lead us. As a journalist and longtime observer of the political scene, Sheehy contends that the Watergate affair of the early 1970s serves as a perfect example of the links between character and leadership. As Richard Nixon demonstrated so well, says Sheehy, "The Presidency is not the place to work out one's personal pathology."

William James believed that the most interesting and important thing about a person, that which determines the person's perspective on the world, is his or her philosophy of life—that is, values, ideals, and beliefs. These are the things a person chooses to hold as dear, important, and/or sacred; they are the road maps that help a person to decipher and explain what James calls the "booming, buzzing confusion" of reality. They are things we are willing to act for and act on. Our philosophy of life is defined by what we choose to value, and our character is defined by actually living out that which we value. James believes that an honest person experiencing hard times will make every effort to sooner or later honor a debt, but that a dishonest person may never repay a debt even if he or she possesses more than sufficient resources to do so.

Ethicist Robert C. Solomon defines virtues as lived behavior traits that contribute to and are essential for achieving happiness, getting along with others, and, in general, living well. For Solomon, like Aristotle, virtues are desirable traits of character, which we choose and make second nature by repetition and habit. Thus virtuous behavior is not an accident or mere luck or a one-time event. A virtuous act is doing the right thing for the right reason, habitually and purposefully. Ethics, says Solomon, is a question of one's whole character, not just a question of one particular virtue or another.

In the *Nicomachean Ethics*, Aristotle offers us a list of virtues that he claims are suitable for the "whole character" of the "great-souled person"—*megalopsuchos*. Although this list has been criticized for being culturally specific and only reflecting Aristotle's idealized version of the Greek gentleman, it has withstood the test of time and, at a minimum, serves as a solid basis for a larger discussion of both male and female public civility and virtuous conduct. Humanities scholar Martha C. Nussbaum of the University of Chicago has created a useful chart that lists the various spheres of human experience that trigger or necessitate a virtuous response.

Spheres of Experience	Virtue
1. Fear of important damages, especially death	Courage
2. Bodily appetites and their pleasures	Moderation
3. Distribution of limited resources	Justice
4. Management of one's personal property, where others are concerned	Generosity
5. Management of personal property, where hospitality is concerned	Expansive Hospitality
6. Attitudes and actions with respect to one's own worth	Greatness of soul
7. Attitude to slights and damages	Mildness of temper
8. Association and living together and the fellowship of words and actions.	
a. Truthfulness in speech	Truthfulness
b. Social association of a playful kind	Easy grace (contrasted with coarseness, rudeness, insensitivity)
c. Social association more generally	Nameless, but a kind of friendliness (contrasted with irritability and grumpiness)
9. Attitude to the good and ill fortune of others	Proper judgment (contrasted with enviousness, spitefulness, etc.)
10. Intellectual life	The various intellectual virtues, such as perceptiveness, knowledge, etc.
11. The planning of one's life and conduct	Practical wisdom

The Rare Virtue of Integrity

It can be argued that moral character is the sum total of our values, virtues, and vices. The Romans had a perfect Latin word to describe and measure the quality of a person's character, *integritas*. Ethically speaking, integrity means "the state or quality of being entire or complete." It means soundness, being unimpaired, having all the component pieces fit together and be whole. It means an attempt to adhere to a cluster of virtues and values that complement and reinforce one another. Integrity is about self-restraint, self-control, self-mastery, or continence.

Integrity is not just about simple addition. Integrity means "living coherently," what the Greek stoics called *homologoumenôs zên*, presenting to the world a sense of self that is not Janus-faced, fractured, or schizophrenic. Integrity is about one's sense of personal identity and honor. It is a matter of integrating the various parts of our personality into a harmonious, intact whole. An integrated character does not do and say one thing when no one else is around and yet another when someone is present. Integrity is something that all morally serious people care about. To describe someone as exhibiting a lack of integrity is to offer a damning judgment. "It carries the implication that this individual is not to be relied upon, that in some fundamental way they are not someone who we can, or should, view as being wholly unequivocally there. The foundations of self and character are not sound; the ordering of values is not coherent."

In his 1996 bestseller, *Integrity*, Stephen L. Carter suggests that integrity is a kind of *uber*-virtue or a type of "philosophical cement" that contains and coordinates all of one's other virtues and values. Carter understands integrity as having the courage of one's convictions. He suggests that if ethics is living out what we value, then the integrity of a person's character, or lack thereof, is as good a yardstick as any to predict ethical conduct. Carter describes integrity as marked by three practices: (1) One takes pains to try to discern what is right from wrong; (2) One is willing to shape one's actions in accord with that discernment, even when it is difficult or painful to do so [as Walter Lippman so eloquently phrased it, "He has honor if he holds himself to an ideal of conduct though it is inconvenient, unprofitable, or dangerous to do so"]; and (3) One is willing to acknowledge publicly what one is doing. In short, a person of integrity is reflective, steadfast, trustworthy, and whole. "A person of integrity," said Carter, "is a whole person, a person somehow undivided."

Character Education

Herbert Spencer said, "Education has for its object the formation of character." Socrates once claimed that "an education in virtue is the only form of education worthy of the title." Michael Josephson, author of *The Power of Character: Prominent Americans Talk about Life, Family, Work, Values, and More*, couldn't agree more. Josephson believes that we

can educate for character and ethics from day one of
a child's school experience. According to Josephson,
"character education" is neither politically incorrect,
pap, philosophical propaganda, or fanatical sectarianism.
Character education consists of six core ethical values that
transcend cultural, religious, as socioeconomic differences.
Josephson is convinced that character education will lead
to a stronger sense of community because it will raise our
awareness and concern for others, and it will help to establish the habits of civility and cooperation.

Trustworthiness: Don't deceive, cheat, or steal. Build a good
reputation. Be reliable.

Respect: Be tolerant of differences and considerate of
other's feelings.

Responsibility: Do what you are supposed to do. Be
accountable. Persevere.

Fairness: Take turns. Share. Play by the rules. Don't take
advantage of others.

Caring: Forgive others. Help people in need. Express gratitude. Be kind.

Citizenship: Obey laws and rules. Respect authority.
Stay informed.

What Does Conscience Really Mean?

According to *Chicago Tribune* columnist Eric Zorn, a person of character is someone who has a conscience. Unfortunately, to most modern ears, says Zorn, the word "conscience" is too abstract, ephemeral, and downright old-fashioned to be used in most conventional conversations. What comes to mind, for a lot of people, is the image of a little person sitting on your shoulder who is whispering in your ear and offering advice and judgment on the moral goodness or blameworthiness of your actions. Nevertheless, Zorn argued, even though the word is rarely used, its meaning, function, and purpose is neither obsolete nor irrelevant.

The term "conscience" implies care for, concern with, or, at the very least, recognition of others. Our conscience is not just a nagging, fault-finding, superego cop. Conscience is from the Latin *conscire*, "to be conscious," "to know." Conscience is the faculty, the power, the instinct, the ability to reflect on, be sensitive to, evaluate, and make judgments about our interactions with others. It is not an infallible instinct. It is not a perfect emotional buzzer that can always distinguish between right and wrong. It is not a perfect truth detector. But if we are lucky, if we are not totally lost in the emotional maze of our own narcissism, conscience at the very least forces us to ponder our relationships with others and to make some sort of judgments about what we consider to be acceptable or unacceptable behavior in their regard.

If character is living out what we value, conscience is its inner counterpart, that part of us that makes judgments and evaluations about, when, how, and with whom that value should or should not be applied. Conscience is frequently the first step in making a moral decision, the internal uneasiness that prompts us to ask ourselves some hard questions, which may well take the shape of the following:

- Is it legal?
- Is it right and fair for others as well as myself?
- Can I truthfully defend my decision to others: family, friends, colleagues?
- Would I feel comfortable seeing my action reported in the news media?
- Can I live with my conscience as well as the consequences of my action?
- Am I treating others in the same way that I would treat myself or people I know and love?

In the words of Carol Gilligan, conscience requires us to listen to "other voices." In 1982 Gilligan published her landmark book, *In a Different Voice: Psychological Theory and Women's Development*. This book contains her claim, against Lawrence Kohlberg (see chap. 2), that women speak about ethics in a voice that is different from that of men. Gilligan argues that because Kohlberg's longitudinal study was based on an all-male sample, Kohlberg did not take into consideration the ways women speak, think, and solve moral problems. Gilligan claims that because Kohlberg's "six stages of moral development" did not take into account "women's voices," his theory is incomplete if not incorrect.

Gilligan does not regard women's and men's respective moralities as being immutably and absolutely separate, but she is convinced that a more complete ethical system must take into account how we are raised and the different ways that boys and girls are socialized to play different roles as men and women. Men, she argued, are socially conditioned to be autonomous, independent, problem solving. Men, therefore, think in terms of logical reasoning, hierarchies, abstract principles, objective notions of duty, and an ethics of justice. Women, on the other hand, are trained to be members of a group, to be co-dependent, caring, compassionate, nurturing. For women, ethics is about equity, not equality; relationships, responsibilities, and caring, not just rules and abstract principles.

It is important to recognize, I think, that Gilligan's critique of Kohlberg and Freud, as well as the prejudicial perspectives of ethics and psychoanalysis that suggest that women are morally and psychologically inferior to men, is much more important than a mere academic debate. To her great credit, Gilligan is not just saying that "women speak a different voice," but that women, raised in a web of relationships, also "listen to different voices." Her point is not just that Kohlberg did not listen to women's voices, and she is not contending that women are better. Rather, her larger message is that for anyone to be ethical, he or she must be open to the voices of others.

In Gilligan's view, caring for others, being responsive to others, and helping others begins with talking and listening to them. According to Gilligan, "the moral person is one who helps others; goodness is service, meeting one's obligations and responsibilities to others." For Gilligan, the most basic moral imperative is the "injunction to care, [the] responsibility to discern and alleviate the 'real and recognizable trouble' of this world." According to Gilligan, we are by nature interdependent, not independent, creatures. We have a responsibility to care for and help others. Because we live in relationships with others, we cannot do nothing. In an ethical predicament, neutrality is unacceptable. In this regard, Gilligan's thinking may echo Dante's in the *Divine Comedy*: "The hottest places in hell are reserved for those who, in a period of moral crisis, maintain their neutrality."

To lift a page from a much older tradition, one might say that Gilligan saw all of us as having a responsibility to be a *mensch*. The word "mensch" (rhymes with bench) is Yiddish (a language written in Hebrew letters with primarily but not exclusively a German vocabulary). A mensch is a person of character, an individual of recognized worth and behavior. James Atlas says a mensch is a person of fundamental decency, a person of high values and standards. A mensch is both compassionate and proactive in her relationships with others. She tries to do the right thing, for the right reason, purposefully. A mensch is not a saint or a hero or always perfect in conduct, but she does always see her life in the context of others and, when necessary, in the service of others. Perhaps, the concept of mensch is best understood by offering an example of its converse. In the words of Mma Precious Ramotswe, the fictional Botswanian female detective of the *No. 1 Ladies Detective Agency* fame, "He was a bad man, a selfish man who never once put himself out for another—not even his wife."

Of course being a mensch is an ongoing activity and not a one-time affair or an episodic experience. Ethical character is formed over time and can withstand the test of time. Aristotle reportedly said, "Never judge a person moral until they are dead." What he meant by that, I think, is that on any given day or moment, we make mistakes. We fail; we act in ways we wish we had not. Who of us is without regret or fault? A person's character must be judged in perspective, over time. Character, like a skill or art form, must be practiced to be perfected and maintained. And yet some mistakes, some actions, some behavior, intended or not, can change our lives and our reputations forever. As Warren Buffet said, "It takes 20 years to build a reputation for character and five minutes to ruin it."

> Sow a thought, and you reap an act;
>
> Sow an act, and you reap a habit;
>
> Sow a habit, and you reap a character;
>
> Sow a character, and you reap a destiny.
>
> **—Samuel Smiles**

4. It's So Easy To Be a Bystander

"I didn't want my husband to get involved," a housewife said.
"We thought it was a lovers' quarrel," said another woman.
"I went back to bed."
"I didn't know," said still another.
"I don't know," said others. . . .
Nobody can say why the thirty-eight did not lift the phone while
Miss Genovese was being attacked, since they cannot say themselves.

—**A. M. Rosenthal**

A. M. Rosenthal wrote in *Thirty-Eight Witnesses,* "In a decade
scarred by some of the worst tragedies in this country's history,
March 13, 1964 stands apart from the other atrocities, not
because of the identity of the victim—whose name was not
Kennedy, King, or Malcolm—but because of the circumstances."
Hundreds of killings occurred in New York City in 1964, and
there were 9,360 murders in the United States that year. But there
was one random street killing that was different, unforgettable,
and almost unbelievable. At about 3:15 A.M. on a brisk winter
morning along a quiet, picturesque, respectable, tree-lined street
in Kew Gardens of Queens, New York City, Catherine "Kitty"

Genovese, the 28-year-old daughter of middle-class Italian-American parents, was brutally stabbed to death. Kitty was a bar manager at Ev's Eleventh Hour Club, a small neighborhood bar, which was about five miles away from an apartment she shared with Mary Ann Zielonko at 82-70 Austin Street. Getting out of her car in the parking lot across the street from where she lived, Kitty realized that a man was following her, and she began to run. Her attacker, Winston Moseley, was bigger and faster. He easily caught up with Kitty, who was just 5'1" and 105 pounds, jumped on her back, pinned her to the ground, and stabbed her several times. For approximately 35 minutes Moseley attacked Kitty three different times and inflicted numerous wounds. She was dead on arrival at Queens General Hospital. But according to the emergency room doctor, the first few knife wounds had not been fatal. What killed her were the 12 or more that she received during the course of her multiple attacks. Frederick Lussen, the assistant chief inspector for the Queens Detectives said, "As we have reconstructed the crime, the assailant had three chances to kill this woman during a thirty-five minute period. If we had been called when he first attacked, this woman might not be dead now."

There are at least three factors that make Kitty Genovese's murder especially heinous and unforgettable. To begin with, it was a random act that occurred without rhyme or reason. Moseley was driving by when Kitty left work and got into her car to drive home. Moseley just followed her. After he was captured, he told police that he "had no reason to kill *her*. . . . I [just] went out that night intending to kill a woman." He said, "I had an uncontrollable urge to kill. . . . When I got such a thought, it remained with me regardless of what else I might be thinking. I had a hunting knife that I had taken from a previous burglary, and I took it with me." In court, Moseley testified that neither robbery nor rape was a primary motivation for his actions, "I just had in mind to kill her." However, at the end, when Kitty lay semiconscious and incoherent, he did cut off her bra and panties and sexually assault her. And he did take $49 out of her wallet. After all, he asked the court, "Why would I throw money away?"

The second startling aspect of this crime was its sheer brutality. In the course of the three separate stabbing events, Kitty endured at least 17 separate wounds. When Moseley first pinned her down, he stabbed her numerous times in the back. The second time, she received multiple wounds in the chest. In the last attack, to stop her screaming, Moseley stabbed her in the neck at least once. Ms. Genovese did not die quickly or easily.

Finally, and most horribly, Kitty Genovese's cries and death agonies were heard or seen by dozens of people living in the apartment buildings surrounding the crime scene. From the moment Kitty began to run, she was calling for help. When Moseley first caught her she screamed, "Oh my God! He stabbed me! Please help me! Please help me!" Lights went on, windows were raised, and a voice called down, "Hey, let that girl alone." The robber walked away and stood in the shadows. When he came back, he started stabbing Kitty again, and she screamed, "I'm dying! I'm dying!" Again lights went on, and windows were opened. Moseley withdrew again and went to move out from under the lights to avoid identification. When he came back, Kitty had made it to the rear of her apartment building. When he found her, by following her trail of blood, Kitty screamed again. "To shut her up," he said, Moseley stabbed her in the neck, reducing her cries to low groans and moaning. Moseley said windows were opened up again, and he even heard a door open, but nothing happened. The yelling stopped, no one came down, and Moseley finished his ugly business and drove away. Moseley later commented, "Oh, I knew they wouldn't do anything. People never do. That late at night, they just go back to sleep."

At about 3:50 A.M., someone who lived in the same building where Genovese lived called the police. But before he did so, he called a friend for advice on whether he should get involved. Within minutes the police arrived to find Kitty's battered and bloody body. After the ambulance left the scene, detectives began to canvass the neighborhood and pieced together a story and a time line that horrified them almost as much as the crime itself. When they added up the pieces, they knew they had at least 38 people who had witnessed the attack on Genovese and had done nothing to help her.

These witnesses said such things as, "It was none of my business," "So many, many [other] times in the night I heard screams," "I'm not the police," "I couldn't make out what she said," "I just saw this guy kneeling over her," "I thought it was some kids having fun," "I thought there must have been 30 calls already," "Frankly, we were afraid." And the saddest one of all: "I was tired."

Chief investigator Bernard Jacobs rebutted all of these excuses with one succinct sentence: "They were in their homes, near phones, why should they be afraid to call the police?" Jacobs conceded that, at the time, there was no law requiring someone witnessing a crime to report it to the police. But, he asked, "shouldn't morality oblige a witness to do so?"

The Genovese Syndrome

Example is the school of mankind and they learn at no other.

—Edmund Burke

The Genovese murder shocked and appalled the world, and in the United States it prompted a soul-searching scrutiny of who we as a people are. It was as if the murder had thrust before us a mirror in which we saw clearly a dark aspect of human nature that we hadn't known existed. Stanley Milgram, a psychologist who was also a native New Yorker, captured the mood—or at least one side of it—perfectly: "The case touched on a fundamental issue of the human condition, our primordial nightmare. . . . If we need help, will those around us stand around and let us be destroyed or will they come to our aid? Are those other creatures out there to help us sustain our life and values, or are we individual flecks of dust just floating around in a vacuum?" A. M. Rosenthal gives the flip side of this "primordial nightmare," which is no less horrifying: "Every man must fear the witness in himself who whispers to close the window."

Psychologists struggled to understand the 38 people who had met Genovese's cries for help with immobile silence, and they increasingly referred to the conditions that they saw as creating that silence as "the Genovese Syndrome," a term now established in professional parlance. Jeff Pearlman, a *Chicago Tribune* reporter, wrote recently, "Four decades after her death, Kitty Genovese is remembered not so much as a human being but as a cultural catch phrase for inexcusable indifference. The term *The Genovese Syndrome* has now become synonymous with the dark side of urban existence. Too often we are too frightened, too alienated, too self absorbed to get involved in helping a fellow human being in dire trouble."

According to psychologists Bibb Latane and John Darley and communications expert Christine Silk, the Genovese Syndrome is a species of a larger psychological phenomenon called the "Bystander Effect." Silk argues that a great deal of human behavior is determined by "social proof." Social proof, she says, simply means that people don't just mindlessly copy what others do, but we do take cues from others when deciding what to do or how to behave in a given situation, especially a novel one. For example, she says, suppose a fire alarm unexpectedly goes off. Chances are, before you go running out the door yelling fire, you'll check out what other people are doing. If you don't smell smoke, and nobody is in a panic, you'll probably assume, along with everyone else, that it's a false alarm. Social proof is a shortcut to acquiring knowledge that can guide our actions. But, says Silk, it is not foolproof and can lead us astray, which is probably what happened in the Genovese incident.

Latane and Darley believe that the notion of social proof is the driving mechanism for the Dependence Effect. In novel, stressful, unusual, dangerous, threatening, or just plain uncomfortable situations, we look around for cues and suggestions from others. The need to do the socially correct thing too often deters us from doing the ethically correct thing. Many of those who witnessed the attacks on Genovese in Kew Gardens said they weren't sure it was a true emergency. Others thought they were witnessing a fight, and they knew that if the people fighting were friends, lovers, or spouses, getting involved could put them in a tricky situation. And since no one else was doing anything, many thought that it was not a true emergency—and hence there was no need for them to get involved. (What's easy to forget in this scenario, of course, is that all the witnesses were looking for social cues from their fellow witnesses; and when no one reacts, nothing gets done.)

Latane and Darley suggest that social proof spawns a state of "pluralistic ignorance" in which each bystander/witness decides that since nobody is concerned, nothing is wrong, and nothing

any attempt to help the victim or to notify the police. Instead, Elaine and George crack jokes about the victim's girth, Kramer videotapes the carjacking, and Jerry doesn't even pause his cell phone conversation while the robbery is going on.

Soon after the incident, the "New York Four" are arrested and charged with breaking Latham's new "Good Samaritan Law," which "requires a person to help or assist anyone in danger as long as it is reasonable to do so." Jerry, Elaine, and Kramer are dumbfounded, and George is narcissistically piqued. "Why would we want to help someone?" he asks. "That's what nuns and Red Cross workers are for."

Thrown into jail and forced to defend themselves, Jerry and company retain the services of Jackie Chiles, a writ-large caricature of the real-life Johnnie "O. J." Cochran, to defend them. To begin with, Chiles claims that the law is "deplorable, unfathomable, and improbable." Both the judge and the jury disagree, and the trial goes forward. Chiles then bases his defense on the premise that his clients did not commit a crime by doing nothing. Doing nothing is nothing. He argues that "you can't be a bystander and be guilty. Bystanders are by definition innocent. That's the nature of bystanding." Besides, Chiles suggests, you can't legislate morality. You can't make people good. In the United States, he says, "you don't even have to help anybody. . . . That's what this country is all about." Once again, the judge and jury disagree. The New York Four are convicted of violating Latham's Good Samaritan Law because, as the judge said, their "callous indifference and utter disregard for everything that is good and decent rocked the foundation on which this society is built."

Although it is true that you cannot make people ethical in their hearts, you can require/force them to act ethically. As a society, we regularly legislate/mandate morality by custom and tradition or the coercion of law and the threat of penalty. State or local laws have sanctions against a number of behaviors that we consider to fall within the realm of morality: murder, theft, adultery, slander, and a number of other things.

Seinfeld's final episode satirically develops a series of serious questions that are at the very heart of the ethical enterprise. Putting aside a consideration of family and friends, what are our obligations to the great sea of others, our neighbors? Are we obligated to help neighbors when doing so is reasonable and does not entail a serious inconvenience or risk of harm? Are we obligated to help neighbors where the price we pay may include the risk of great danger and/or inconvenience? Are we required to endanger ourselves for our neighbors? Finally, do we at least have minimal duties to help our neighbors? Is there such a thing as a minimally decent Samaritan?

A certain man went down from Jerusalem to Jericho, and fell among thieves, which stripped him of his raiment, and wounded him, and departed, leaving him half dead.

And by chance there came down a certain priest that way,
and when he saw him, he passed by on the other side.

And likewise a Levite, when he was at the place, came and
looked on him, and passed by on the other side.

But a certain Samaritan, as he journeyed, came where he
was; and when he saw him he had compassion on him.

And went to him, and bound up his wounds pouring in oil
and wine, and set him on his own beast, and brought him
to an inn, and took care of him.

And on the morrow, when he departed, he took out two
pence, and gave them to the host, and said unto him,
"Take care of him, and whatsoever thou spendest more,
when I come again, I will repay thee."

—Luke 10: 29–39

When Jesus of Nazareth was asked, "Who is my neighbor?"
he responded with the parable of the good Samaritan. There
are a number of issues that make this parable both powerful
and problematic. The first bystander is a man of God, a man
of the people of God, a priest, presumable a rabbi. And yet he
couldn't be bothered, he didn't stop. The second bystander was a
Levite, a person from the house of Levi, a member of the Jewish
aristocracy. This nobleman by custom and birth paused, looked,
and passed on, leaving the injured man to his fate. Both of these

bystanders are solid members of the community, members of the established social and moral order, and yet they do not help. The power and the irony of this tale is that it is a Samaritan—a low-caste, socially marginal, and a non-kosher or unclean (*pareve*) member of the community—who stops and ministers to the needs of this stranger/neighbor. And not only does he offer immediate assistance, he arranges, at his own expense, for a period of extended assistance after he is gone.

Scholars and ethicists have long debated about the exact meaning of the parable. Jesus tersely said, "Go and do thou likewise." But what does that really suggest? Is there an absolute standard I must meet? Must I help anyone, everyone I see in peril and in need? Must I give something to every beggar I encounter? Must I open my house to orphans? Must I give all or most of my distributive income to needy charities and causes? Must I be my brother's keeper, no matter what the price? Common sense suggests that such an interpretation is too severe. Rather, is the Galilean saying that the parable is a moral metaphor rather than a prescription for specific actions and absolute obligations? Is the main message of the story the nonspecific but nonetheless obligatory injunction that all others (our literal and figurative brothers and neighbors) are "owed something more than just being left alone"? Attention must be paid! Something must be done! Doing nothing is something. Doing nothing makes us co-responsible. It is allowing and permitting the situation to happen. It is sanctioning the nongood by doing no good, no thing. In fact, to do nothing is to assist in the deed. As William James suggested, "The only thing necessary for evil to prevail is for good men to do nothing." Although the bottom line is rarely clear as to what we should do exactly, I think the bottom line still nevertheless requires us to do something. As ethicist Amitai Etzioni persuasively put the point,

> The exclusive pursuit of one's self-interest is not even a good prescription for conduct in the marketplace; for no social, political, economic, or moral order can survive that way. Some measure of caring, sharing, and being our brother's and sister's keeper is essential if we are not all to fall back on an ever more expansive government, bureaucratized welfare agencies, and swollen regulations, police, courts, and jails.

Genocides: Perpetrators and Victims

> This was the thing that I had wanted to understand ever since the war. Nothing else. How a human being can remain indifferent. . . . Those who were permanently and merely spectators—all those were closed to me, incomprehensible.
>
> **—Elie Wiesel,** *The Town Beyond the Wall*

It has been argued that next to the U.S. Civil War, World War II is the most written about and the most documented war in history. A significant and especially horrifying part of this conflict was the Nazi strategy to solve the "Jewish Problem," *Judenfrage*. Though complicated and convoluted in its political and cultural evolution and roots, the Nazis' Final Solution

Project, *Endlosungsprojekt*, was brutally simple: the systematic extermination of the Jewry of Europe. From Hitler's earliest pamphlets on the "Jewish Problem" to the Nuremberg Laws of 1935 that stripped Jewish aliens, *Fremdkorper*, of their citizenship to the Wannsee Conference held in Berlin in 1942, which put pen to paper and put the machinery of death to work throughout Europe, Nazi propaganda preached the credo that the total eradication of the subhuman Jews (*untermenschen*) was a necessary condition for final German victory and world hegemony. In *Hitler's Willing Executioners*, which is terrifying if it's true, and still frightening if only partially true, Daniel Jonah Goldhagen maintains that the Nazi elite may have designed the Final Solution, but it was the German people who (willingly?) carried it out.

Goldhagen argues that in the land of Bach, Goethe, Schiller, Kant, and Hegel, the Holocaust happened because the vast majority of the German population either believed in, accepted, or, at the very least, did not challenge the Nazi Party line: *Die Juden find unfer Ungluck* ("The Jews are our misfortune"). Goldhagen suggests that many Germans actively participated in various phases of the Final Solution because they believed in a pure German people (*Volk*) and a pure German Christendom (*deutsche Christenheit*). Some Germans, he said, agreed with the Nazi propaganda campaign but did not participate in its excesses or abuses. They were simply passive bystanders to the horrors of the Holocaust. Goldhagen would hold all of these people as being equally accountable and guilty for the horrors of the Holocaust.

A painful irony that emerges in the Nazi campaign to eradicate the Jews as a people were those Nazis who were active participants in the Holocaust and yet claimed bystander status. A case in point was Adolf Eichmann. Yes, said Eichmann, I facilitated the Final Solution. Yes, I organized the railroads and the transportation system to accommodate the death trains destined for the concentration camps all around Europe. Yes, I tabulated the numbers, kept the books, managed the system that attempted to eliminate a whole category of people. But, said Eichmann, it was not personal. I did not want to do it. I had no free will in this matter. I was the "involuntary agent of an impersonal force." I only did my duty.

In the book he wrote awaiting execution in Israel in 1962, titled *Know Thyself*, Eichmann claims that intellectually and at the level of strict intent, he was but a pawn, a bureaucratic bystander in a larger process. "I myself was unable to jump over my own shadow," he wrote. "I was only a tool in the hands of stronger powers."

There is, sadly, yet another category of bystanders in the Holocaust drama. This group, however, is to be pitied rather than condemned. This is a group of individuals who were bystanders to themselves. This group of bystanders were those who could not believe what was going to happen to them even when it became clear that it indeed was really going to happen.

These were the people for whom denial was preferable to reality. These were the hundreds of thousands, if not millions, of starving, sleep-deprived, physically maltreated, emotionally spent Jews from all over Europe who, like zombies and sleepwalkers, marched to their own deaths without a great deal of struggle or debate. These were the people for whom, in an environment of fear and displacement, were stripped of their sense of self and disabled by their feeling of impotence and despair. Elie Wiesel writes that in the spring of 1944, people were confident that Germany was being beaten. "'Hitler won't be able to do us any harm, even if he wants to,'" people were saying. "Yes, we even doubted that he wanted to exterminate us. . . . Was he going to wipe out a whole people? . . . So many millions! . . . And in the middle of the twentieth century!" Shortly afterward, Wiesel and his family were taken to concentration camps, where most of his family died.

Mark C. Ross, a veteran African safari guide, gives a gripping and vivid account of what it means to be a "bystander to oneself," even when you don't want to be. On March 1, 1999, Mark was camped with four of his clients in Uganda in search of endangered mountain silver-back gorillas. By day's end, two of his clients and six other tourists had been murdered by Hutu rebels who had crossed over the Congo border. Kept as a hostage and not knowing if he or his other guests would be killed, Mark felt himself falling into a "tunnel of fear." "Sitting on the lawn at camp," he said, "surrounded by rampaging human beings and knowing that at any instant any one of us could be shot in the back of the head, I was losing my feelings in my body." He said his "sense of touch was almost numb" and his "sense of hearing muted." He even lost his sense of color and depth perception. He knew, he said, he was slipping. He knew he was losing control and falling into a dangerous state of shock. But he also knew that he could not shut down. If he did, he was sure he would forfeit whatever chance he had of saving himself and his clients. But, he said, it would have been so easy to give in to his shock and fear. It would have been so easy to give up and be a spectator to his own demise.

We've all seen a film, a play, a TV show, where the "bad guys" do terrible things to an individual, and no one tries to stop them or help the injured party. But it doesn't have to be just about "bad guys" doing terrible things. It's also about the little banalities and courtesies in life. It's about the general unwillingness to step outside the shadow of self. Doing the right thing always involves some risk, always involves taking a chance, always involves extending ourselves for others. Let's be honest: It's hard to be a hero or to even just be of help to another. It's easier to look away, walk away, pretend you didn't notice. It's easier to lie to yourself by repeating again and again, "It's really none of my business."

5. Change, Choice, and Culture

Suppose your great-great-grandparents, who lived four generations ago, materialized in America of the present day. Surely they would first be struck by the scale and clamor of twenty-first century living. The physical speed of contemporary life would also shock them. . . . Yet as your ancestors learned more about how we live, they would be dazzled. Unlimited food at affordable prices . . . ; college as the common destination of the young . . . ; medical progress that in a century has increased the average life span (by 35 years) . . . ; the end of backbreaking physical toil for most wage earners; the advent of instantaneous global communication and same-day travel to distant cities; home ownership for the majority. . . . All told, your great-great-grandparents might say modern America is the realization of Utopia.

—Gregg Easterbrook, *The Progress Paradox*

How many times in a conversation with a parent or older friend have you heard one of the following phrases: "When I was a kid . . . ," "When I was your age . . . ," or "When I went to school . . . ,"? Implicit in all of these statements is the notion that things were different back then and that times have changed. Well, guess what? They're right! Change is real. And whether it's good, bad, or ugly, change is a natural and continuous process in life. Change is neither an aberration nor a personal assault. As Jean-Paul Sartre would say, "*Merde* just happens!" (For you Latin scholars, that would, of course, be *stercus accidit* or "s__ t happens.") The reality is, change does alter, augment, and restructure the world around us. Change affects the currency and credibility of our ideas and values. Change also forces us to reevaluate or at least revisit some of our long-held beliefs and convictions.

It would, of course, be easy or, at least, a lot easier to make decisions—ethical or otherwise—if they occurred in a vacuum free of variables, without change or outside influence. But clearly, such is not the case. And so the challenge all of us face is to try to cope with change while managing our ethical priorities and moral sense of self.

> Reality is mobility . . . only changing states exist. Rest is never more than apparent, or, rather, relative.
>
> **—Henri Bergson**

Twenty-five hundred years ago, when the iron hoe was an important new invention in the world, the pre-Socratic philosophers of Greece conjectured on the metaphysical substructure of reality. For Pythagoros, math was the logic, language, and glue of the cosmos. For Thales, the stuff of life was water. For Anaximenes, it was air. For Anaximander, it was the forces of hot and cold. And for Heraclitus, the fundamental element of life was change. Heraclitus noted that nothing is permanent; flux or change is everywhere. Reality is flux, permanency is not possible, and the only constant is change.

Heraclitus

The river where you set

your foot just now is gone—

those waters giving way to this,

(and) now this.

Fragment #41

The sun is new again,

each day.

Fragment #32

Even if change does not constitute the metaphysical and philosophical building blocks of reality, psychologically Heraclitus's general thesis is compelling and seemingly self-evident to both reason and the senses. If things are always changing, if nothing is ever final or fixed, then all of life, all of truth, is not necessarily relative but is in process, evolution, and development. If change is the essential activity of experience, then all that we witness and know is continuously being redefined, reshaped, and even altered. Change does not mean that there is *no thing*. It does mean that all leveraged buyouts, hostile takeover bids, women in the workplace, or gay marriages. Each generation in turn finds itself confronted with issues and ideas that preceding generations never imagined. Each generation must address the issues of its age, often using vocabularies of thought and methodologies specifically created to confront the issue at hand. As Albert Einstein so eloquently phrased it, "The significant problems we face cannot be solved at the same level of thinking we were at when we created them."

Directly connected to the problem of the increasing pace and rate of change in our lives is the increasing number and variety of choices we are forced to make in our lives. Albert Camus once asked the question, "Should I kill myself, or have a cup of coffee?" I believe that this quote is nothing more than a dramatic, tongue-in-cheek, existential reminder that everything we do in life is a choice, and that all of human existence and our very essence (our definition as a person) is literally defined by the choices we make.

Clearly, one need not be a card-carrying existentialist to agree with Camus on this point. Life *is* full of choices. Some of the choices we face are critical, and many more of them are utterly unimportant. But choose we must. We are, in fact, a species of choosers, and we are known and defined by the quality of the choices we make.

As social theorist Barry Schwartz writes in his recent bestseller *The Paradox of Choice: Why More Is Less*, choices and choosing are psychologically a crucial part of the human condition. Making choices and the freedom to make choices is how human beings express their autonomy, develop self-respect and self-worth, and achieve self-definition. Freedom of choice is a core value politically as well, says Schwartz. The United States was founded on a commitment to individual freedom and autonomy. Politically and economically, freedom allows people to choose, to risk, to take a chance, to extend themselves to improve the quality of their lives. According to Schwartz, people want and need to direct their own lives. Choices keep us growing, and offer us the possibilities of creature comforts, greater levels of awareness, and creativity. When there are no choices, life can become uniform, utterly uninteresting, and unbearable.

But, says Schwartz, when the number of choices keeps *growing*, there is a downside. He argues that just because *some* choice is good, it doesn't mean that *more* choice is always better. Too many choices can lead to overload, anxiety, stress, dissatisfaction, bad decision making, and even clinical depression. For Schwartz, at some point, too many choices no longer liberates but, rater, debilitates. In fact, too many choices can tyrannize our lives.

Schwartz says that he started his research on the burden of choice when he innocently went into Gap to buy a pair of jeans. He said, "I want a pair of jeans—32–27." The saleswoman said: "Slim fit? Easy fit? Relaxed fit? Baggy or extra baggy? Do you want stonewashed? Or how about unwashed or acid wash? Do you want them faded or regular? How about a button-fly or a zipper-fly?" He said, "Huh? I just want regular jeans. You know, the kind that used to be the only kind." She said, "Regular jeans? Let me go ask somebody."

The problem, Schwartz writes, isn't just this particular choice over that particular choice. The problem is that we now face more choices and decisions today than ever before, and that the cumulative effect of all these added choices demands too much of our time, attention, and energy. It is also the case, says Schwartz, that new choices, more choices, simply present new things to worry about, to master, or perhaps just another thing to get wrong and not even enjoy. (For example, most of us over the age of 40 need a teenager in order to program the VCR or reset the clock!)

From an ethical point of view, true freedom cannot be equated with a surfeit of options and choices. True freedom, or the primary purpose of freedom, is about making good choices about things that really matter. Yes, quotidian choices must be made. It's important to choose a good breakfast cereal, a dependable VCR, an effective household soap, an efficient showerhead, and a trustworthy health insurance policy. But when we must choose from 250 cereals, 400 VCRs, 40 soaps, 35 showerheads, and 500 policies—we find ourselves not only exhausted but disengaged and distracted from more important decisions and choices in our lives. As Schwartz sagely suggests, time spent dealing with consumer choices and ephemeral choices of all kinds is time taken away from choosing to be a good friend, a good spouse, a good parent, or a good person.

What Schwartz's book suggests to me is that too many of the choices we make within our capitalistic culture lock us into a purely parochial and self-serving perspective on reality. These choices reinforce our narcissistic tendencies and insulate us from others. Over time, the volume of choices that we face can anesthetize us to any issue that stands outside of the shadow of self. In the pursuit of too many choices, we are diminished and incomplete. In our preoccupation with self-aggrandizement, we lose ourselves in choices that contribute little or nothing to the matters that truly nourish us, enhance our self-respect, or enable us to participate in community life.

Martin Heidegger, in his philosophical critique of the human condition, *Being and Time*, suggested that in lieu of being able to address the serious choices, questions, and issues in life, we often busy ourselves in idle play, cocktail party conversations, and/or escapist behavior. In American society, of course, the escapist behavior of choice is shopping. In this society we "communicate with commodities." People find comfort in and recognize themselves in their possessions. The seductive siren call of the ad cult industry continually bombards us with a message which is both mystic and metaphysical: "Can't figure out the ultimate questions in life? Done sweat it! We've got it figured out for you. You can buy happiness. You can be loved. You can be accepted. You can be transformed into the person you want to be. Just get our product, and keep buying our product until we come up with another product you will want and need."

Vaclav Havel, the former Czechoslovakian president and playwright, warns us of the spiritual and moral disease engendering worldwide following. Jazz clubs and recordings can be found from New York hot spots to rural outdoor clubs in New Zealand. And yet, jazz is a passion for only a small minority of music lovers. The motion picture industry and television, on the other hand, have cultivated and captured a vast worldwide constituency.

From the onset, the movie industry set out to produce a product that would appeal to a mass audience. Its pitch was never to the discriminating rich with their theater productions and high art. Rather, the industry sought out those who could at least afford a nickel (the price of admission to a nickelodeon). In 1913, *American Movie Magazine* eloquently described what movies meant to early audiences. "It is an art democratic, art for the race. It is in a way a new universal language, even more elemental than music." Statistics gathered in 1907 tell us that more than 200,000 people a day attended New York's 500 movie houses. Contemporary statistics on moviegoing no longer count the number of individuals who attend; rather, they calculate the dollar amount of tickets sold. For example, in 2002 the premier weekend of *Spider-Man* at more than 1,200 theaters nationwide grossed in excess of $114 million. And in the summer of 2004, *Spider-Man 2* earned in excess of $192 million in a Wednesday-through-Sunday opening.

Whether serious dramas, tear-jerker melodramas, action adventures, or musicals, movies historically have offered

Top Worldwide Box Office Sales (in millions of U.S. dollars)

Rank	Domestic	Overseas	World	Titles (1990–2004)
1	$600.8	$1234.6	$1835.4	*Titanic* (1997)
2	$375.7	$752.2	$1127.9	*The Lord of the Rings: The Return of the King* (2003)
3	$317.6	$658.2	$975.8	*Harry Potter and the Sorcerer's Stone* (2001)
4	$431.1	$494.4	$925.5	*Star Wars: Episode I The Phantom Menace* (1999)
5	$341.7	$583.0	$924.7	*The Lord of the Rings: The Two Towers* (2001)
6	$357.1	$563.0	$920.1	*Jurassic Park* (1993)
7	$262.0	$604.4	$866.4	*Harry Potter and the Chamber of Secrets* (2002)
8	$313.8	$546.9	$860.7	*The Lord of the Rings: The Fellowship of the Ring* (2001)
9	$339.7	$513.5	$853.2	*Finding Nemo* (2003)
10	$306.2	$505.0	$811.2	*Independence Day* (1996)
11	$403.7	$403.0	$806.7	*Spider-Man* (2002)
12	$461.0	$337.0	$798.0	*Star Wars* (1977)
13	$328.4	$459.0	$787.4	*The Lion King* (1994)
14	$434.9	$321.8	$756.7	*E.T. the Extra-Terrestrial* (1982)
15	$281.5	$454.2	$735.7	*The Matrix Reloaded* (2003)

Source: http://www.worldwideboxoffice.com

diversion. We wanted a break from the usual. We wanted to be entertained. And in bad times, we wanted to lose ourselves. For the price of admission, we could get lost in the magic of a movie and insulate ourselves from the troubles of the real world. In many theaters across the United States from the Depression eternal struggle between good and evil. It was the stuff that ancient myths and great operas were made of. But it was our stuff, our homegrown mythology, our homemade *Grande ol' Opere*.

Of course, not all westerns attempted to be, or presented themselves as, mythic playlets about right and wrong, good and evil. Like every other genre in film, westerns ran the spectrum of dramatic possibilities. At one end was the politically correct, non-offensive, family acceptable, and cartoonish violence of America's two favorite singing cowboy dandies—Gene Autry (his real name) and Roy Rogers (real name: Leonard Slye). Also included in this category of cowboy stars is my personal favorite, Hopalong Cassidy (real name: William Boyd), or Hoppy to his fans. Handsome, polite, courageous, always in impeccably pressed trousers and shirt, Hoppy kept the bad guys at bay in 41 films at Paramount and 25 films at United Artists before shifting to television in the early 1950s. We loved our cowboy heroes and often tried to emulate their deeds and creeds.

The American Cowboy Commandments

1. The Cowboy must never shoot first, hit a smaller man or take unfair advantage.

2. He must never go back on his word or a trust confided in him.

3. He must always tell the truth.

4. He must be gentle with children, the elderly and animals.

5. He must not advocate or possess racially or religiously intolerant ideas.

6. He must help people in distress.

7. He must be a good worker.

8. He must keep himself clean in thought, speech, action and personal habits.

9. He must respect women, parents, and his nation's laws.

10. The Cowboy is a patriot.

—**Gene Autry**, *Cowboy Creed*, **1939**

Strategically occupying the center and soul of the cowboy genre was John "Duke" Wayne (real name: Marion Michael Morrison). From his first big break in *The Big Trail* (1930) through his Academy Award–winning performance in *True Grit* (1969), John Wayne was the embodiment of the American cowboy. It was as if he were born to play the characters that Louis L'Amour created in his novels and short stories. Wayne's gestures, his walk, his smile, the way he wore his hat or said hello became the personification of what we thought a cowboy should be. His name was transformed from a proper noun to a verb or, more precisely, a state of mind. Entire generations of moviegoers were raised on the "cult of Wayneism" or the "John Wayne thing." Wayne communicated a certain male mystique and a model of manhood that was both chivalric and brutalizing. Wayne's characters, whether in westerns or military action films, were a combination of rugged individualism, quiet courage, and a strong sense of justice, order, discipline, and loyalty. At countless Saturday afternoon matinees, "The Duke" taught us to honor our word, do our duty, fight off fear, demonstrate physical courage, and, if need be, kill without sentiment or remorse. In a career that spanned 47 years, The Duke became an institution as well as a star. I do not think its outrageous to claim that he was as much a symbol for American democracy as Uncle Sam.

At the other end of the spectrum was something loosely referred to as the "adult western." These were supposed to be examples of serious drama or psychological thrillers, but set in the West. Films such as *Ox-Bow Incident* (1941), *Shane* (1953), *High Noon* (1952), *One-Eyed Jacks* (1961), *The Man Who Shot Liberty Valence* (1962), *Little Big Man* (1971), *The Unforgiven* (1992), and, most recently, *Open Range* (2003), are all westerns to be assured, but they are a far cry from the almost clownish antics of Gene and Roy. Nevertheless, high art or low, for well over 50 years, cowboy films were hot at the box office and almost guaranteed cash in the bank for the moviemakers who produced them.

I believe that the American public's enjoyment of crime films, gangster stories, and mob movies comes out of our infatuation with cowboy films. In some sense, mob films are urban updates of our love affair with the West. Interestingly enough, in 1905 the Edison company also cranked out one of the earliest crime films, *Desperate Encounters between Burglars and Police.* In many ways we are entertained by the exploits of mob guys for the same reason that we like cowboys. We seem to be drawn to their sense of rugged individualism, their resourcefulness, and their eagerness to take risks, be experimental, push the envelope, be different. We wonder at their daring, their cheek, their flare for the outrageous. We are, I think, envious of their ability to break with convention and to do things their own way.

There is nothing particularly new in any of this. We have long loved the rough, the rascal, the "bad boy" in both our films and our literature. Of course, our infatuation with these bad boys and "pirate kings" has its limits. We do not want nor are we easily drawn, in fiction or in fact, to antiheroes who are sadists, serial killers, or ghouls. Antiheroes need to be both scary and lovable; they need to find a balance between being naughty and nice, tough and soft, strong and yet compassionate.

Before *The Godfather, Part I*, mob films were predominately, but not exclusively, about non-Italian urban bad guys. They were gangsters with Irish, German, English, "everyman" Caucasian faces. And even the stars of these films, different from most of the cast of *The Sopranos*; *The Godfather, Parts I, II,* and *III*; and *Goodfellas*, were anything but Italian: James Cagney, George Raft, Humphrey Bogart, Edward G. Robinson, and Paul Muni. According to film historians, the gangster genre before 1930 was made up of mostly B-films, or minor productions, full of poor dialogue, gratuitous violence, and semi-slapstick action scenes, and they were peopled with inept district attorneys, dimwitted cops, and lots of kindhearted ladies of leisure. As one *New York Times* critic wrote in 1928, "When earth's last gangster picture fades from the screen, it may . . . be a relief to more than one person." In 1930, three films were made that helped to redefine a rather underwhelming genre: *Little Caesar*, *The Public Enemy*, and *Scarface*. In comparison to the films that preceded them, these three films were not "gaudy, wine-women-and-machine gun romances." By the standards of their day, these films were almost like documentaries in their realism. The main characters had *gravitas* and were believable. There was a real story line. The dialogue, though stilted and without a trace of obscenity, was engaging and oftentimes gripping. And in most of these films, there was a resolve that was both dramatically satisfying and morally acceptable to their audiences—that is, the bad guys got their just deserts. Moreover, the main actors in these features—Edward G. Robinson, James Cagney, and Paul Muni— achieved almost overnight star status. Critic Lincoln Kirstein proclaimed that the newfound American idol was no longer the western lawman, but a "short red-headed" Irish gangster, James Cagney. "No one," said Kirstein, "expresses more clearly in terms of pictorial action, the delights of violence, the overtones of a semiconscious sadism, the tendency toward destruction, toward anarchy, which is the basis of American sex appeal."

Between 1930 and 1971, a lot of gangland and mobster films were made. Some of them were utterly forgettable, and others can claim a cult following. Some of them had a serious story to tell, and others simply titillated our more prurient side with graphic and prolonged depictions of cruelty, violence, and sexuality. Some were about the cash and the crime, some were about the criminal. A lot of them were *noir* action thrillers, full of characters meticulously dressed in "gangster uniforms" (fedora hats, suits with wide lapels, and light ties and dark shirts), sneering at the camera, and occasionally bursting out into a semi-crazed Tommy Udo laugh (Richard Widmark, *Kiss of Death*). At bottom, most of them were basically stories about tough guys out to beat the system or tough guys who end up beaten by the system.

In one magic movie moment, Francis Ford Coppola in *The Godfather, Part I* (1972), completely transformed the formulaic and somewhat pedestrian antics of gangster flicks into a serious genre that gave mythic, metaphysical, and moral status to Italian mobsters and wise guys. This transformation was, of course, cemented into permanent place (pun intended) with Martin Scorsese's *Goodfellas* (1990), and *Casino* (1995), and the much later stunning contribution of English director Mike Newell, *Donnie Brasco* (1997).

Yes, Coppola's *Godfather* series is full of thievery, violence, and the machinations of Mafia life, but at the same time these obvious story lines are not the only theses or the only agenda of the films. These films were about Machiavelli's analysis of power and the important role of the Prince (the boss, ruler, CEO, or Don) in the life of any organization. These films are about the importance of family and the dynamics of family life, and not just about the concepts of duty and respect in regard to *La Famiglia*. They are films about struggling to achieve personal honor, pride, and respect in life in general and not just about achieving the status of a "made man" in the mob. Like the mystery novels of Scott Turow, P. D. James, and Ruth Rendell, the murder and the mayhem depicted in these movies are often ancillary to the mores and manners that triggered these incidences. And finally, like Mario Puzo's earlier novel, *The Fortune Pilgrim*, these films are about the immigrant experience and what it means to be a "stranger in a strange land." We watched these films. We loved these films. They became part of our moral fabric. They helped us interpret the world and had an impact on how we made choices—ethical and otherwise.

The Small Screen

For all the impact that movies have had on the culture and mores of American life, the medium that has transformed how we live, how we learn, and what we know is, of course, television. Invented in 1925, perfected and commercialized after World War II, television helped to shape America's collective postmodern psyche. In 1948, only 10 percent of American households owned a television. By 1954, thanks in no small part to Milton Berle, Luci and Dezi Arnez, and Bishop Fulton J. Sheen, televisions were in 70 percent of American households.

Media critic Neil Postman contends that the surest way to understand a culture is to understand its tools of communication. He posits that in the second half of the twentieth century, we have shifted from being a typographic to a videographic society.

That is, we no longer search for or gather information from the printed page, but from the images and sound bites of television and, ever increasingly, the computer. According to Postman, the most commonly shared cultural experience in America today is watching television. He suggests that television may be the primary medium by which most of us seek entertainment, gain information, or just relax. It is also, he writes, "our culture's principle mode of knowing about ourselves. Therefore, how television stages the world becomes the mold for how the world is understood and should be staged."

The U.S. Ranks 49th in literacy.

60% of the U.S. population has never read a book.

Only 6% of the U.S. population reads a book a year.

120 million Americans are illiterate or only read at a
fifth grade level.

Only 31% of American readers between the ages of 21 and
35 read the daily paper.

—**Morris Berman,** *The Twilight of American Culture*

Household televisions are turned on, even if not closely watched, an average of 7.6 hours per day. They are closely watched for an average of more than four hours per day. Forty percent of us watch television while eating dinner, and 25 percent of us fall asleep with the television on. One-year-olds in the United States are "babysat" by a television an average of more than six hours a week, and school-age children spend 1,023 hours a year in front of the television. If these statistics are true, it means that today's average child could spend ten years of his or her life watching television. An even more depressing possibility is that two of the ten years that most adults will spend during their lifetimes watching television will be spent watching commercials.

Media watcher Cherly Pawlowski makes the startling claim that more American households have televisions than have indoor plumbing. According to a recent report in the *New York Times*, 98 percent of American households own at least one television, and 40 percent own three or more televisions. Moreover, private ownership of televisions is not limited to our living rooms. Car, cab, and sport utility vehicle manufacturers started offering backseat televisions in 1999, and according to the Consumer Electronics Association, more than 400,000 "mobile video units" were installed in 2002. Televisions have taken over our public lives as well. Some banks and supermarkets have installed them in cashier and checkout lines. Airports, railway, and bus stations have them prominently displayed everywhere. Some restaurants and bars (but not coffeehouses— they, at least for now, are reserved for low platform information systems: music, books, magazines, and newspapers) have televisions strategically placed to better keep their customers entertained, informed, or at least distracted while they wait.

And, let's not forget, no matter where we are or what we're doing—we can always access our favorite TV show or movie on our laptops or by using portable DVD players.

> Here's one more fascinating factoid that demonstrates the pervasiveness and cultural impact of TVs on our lives: According to the *Chicago Tribune*, the 2004 NFL Super Bowl was televised in 229 countries from Austria to Zimbabwe and broadcast in 21 languages. In the United States alone, an estimated 90 million people watched the game.

Again, to reiterate my thesis, we are a media-saturated society and the types of media we are exposed to affects our moral language, our moral perspective on the world, and helps to define our moral options and alternatives. For example, in the past, many of us learned some of our first lessons in manners and morals by watching *Sesame Street*: cooperate, play fair, share things, don't hit people, say you're sorry when you hurt somebody. Today, in watching *The Sopranos*, about 11 million of us per episode are taking a virtual, voyeuristic, X-rated course (containing adult language violence, an occasional dismemberment, nudity, and explicit sex) about the self-defined universe of Mafia ethics: What is duty? What is honor? What is *Omerta*?

TV Guide's List of the 50 Greatest Shows of All Time (2002)

1. "Seinfeld," 1989
2. "I Love Lucy," 1951
3. "The Honeymooners," 1955
4. "All in the Family," 1971
5. "The Sopranos," 1999
6. "60 Minutes," 1968
7. "The Late Show with David Letterman," 1993
8. "The Simpsons," 1989
9. "The Andy Griffith Show," 1960
10. "Saturday Night Live," 1975
11. "The Mary Tyler Moore Show," 1970
12. "The Tonight Show Starring Johnny Carson," 1962
13. "The Dick Van Dyke Show," 1961
14. "Hill Street Blues," 1981
15. "The Ed Sullivan Show," 1948
16. "The Carol Burnett Show," 1967
17. "Today Show," 1952
18. "Cheers," 1982
19. "thirtysomething," 1987
20. "St. Elsewhere," 1982
21. "Friends," 1994
22. "ER," 1994
23. "Nightline," 1980
24. "Law & Order," 1990
25. "M*A*S*H," 1972
26. "The Twilight Zone," 1959
27. "Sesame Street," 1969
28. "The Cosby Show," 1984
29. "Donahue," 1970
30. "Your Show of Shows," 1950
31. "The Defenders," 1961
32. "American Family," 1973
33. "Playhouse 90," 1958
34. "Frasier," 1993
35. "Roseanne," 1988
36. "The Fugitive," 1963
37. "The X-Files," 1993
38. "The Larry Sanders Show," 1992
39. "The Rockford Files," 1974
40. "Gunsmoke," 1955
41. "Buffy the Vampire Slayer," 1997
42. "Rowan & Martin's Laugh-In," 1968
43. "Bonanza," 1959
44. "The Bob Newhart Show," 1972
45. "Twin Peaks," 1990
46. "Star Trek: The Next Generation," 1987
47. "Rocky and His Friends," 1961
48. "Taxi," 1978
49. "The Oprah Winfrey Show," 1986
50. "Bewitched," 1964

When I was a child, there was a Saturday afternoon TV show that few children missed, *Superman*. Even though it was badly written and acted, shot in black and white, produced on an old and weathered soundstage, and had terrible special effects, we loved it! And yes, some children made their own capes, jumped out of a window, and tried to fly just like Superman. Sadly, quite a few of them were injured and a number of them were killed. It is also true that war films such as *To Hell and Back* (1955) and *The Halls of Montezuma* (1951) generated an increase in military enlistments. Cecil B. DeMille's epic *The Ten Commandments* (1956) encouraged an increase in vocations and weekly attendance at churches and synagogues. And in 2004, Mel Gibson's *The Passion of the Christ* was the lead story in many daily papers and magazines, and it fostered nationwide debates on the meaning and purpose of Christ's crucifixion and death.

Though my favorite TV shows and these films were a catalyst for various kinds of behavior—some rational and some not—we are not talking about "mind control," or a pandemic of "monkey-see-monkey-do" aberrant operant conditioning. Although there is a growing body of research that claims to prove a direct relationship between excessive hours in front of TV and a wide range of cognitive problems, including attention deficit disorder, there is no credible research, to date, that demonstrates a strict correlation between what we witness in the media and any specific changes that occur in our personal and public standards of morality and behavior.

I would, nevertheless, argue that although the influence never exactly determines what we think and do, films and TV do change us, wear us down, desensitize us, and make the unusual and the formally unacceptable more palatable or, at least, more commonplace. Like commercials and advertisements, through the sheer function of repetition and exposure, the various messages of the media have the ability to reinforce, modify, or radically change standards and behavior. Just think for a moment how standards have been altered over the last 25 years in regard to language, acceptable levels of violence, nudity, and sex scenes in the movie industry. In David Mamet's *Glengarry Glen Ross* (1992), I stopped counting the use of the F word after 168 times. And in *Taking Lives* (2004), starring Angelina Jolie, the sex and violence left nothing for the imagination to fill in.

> Intimacy doesn't necessarily breed discontent. But saturation and repetition, more often than not, can and will unconsciously undermine the status quo.
>
> **—Ray Benton, marketing analyst**

7. Ethics and the Workplace

"You can't eat for eight hours a day, nor drink for eight hours a day—all you can do for eight hours is work! Which is the reason man makes himself and everybody else so miserable and unhappy."

—William Faulkner

No one is neutral about the topic of work. As adults, work occupies our lives. There is, in fact, nothing more we do with our lives than work. We will not sleep as much, recreate as much, spend as much time with family and friends as we will work. Perhaps that is why we tend to indulge our children when we send them off to college. College is, after all, a fantasyland where days begin at 10:30 A.M. sharp, where evening classes are seen as optional, where the weekend begins on Thursday afternoon, and where summers are off. But after graduation, adultland begins every day at 8 A.M., attendance is not optional, weekends begin Saturday night (if you're lucky), and summers bring no pause in work. Given the amount of time we put in on the job, it is impossible to avoid being affected by the work we do. The ethos (culture) and the ethics of the workplace have an influence on us both on and off the job. In the end, for many of us, truth and ethics becomes what happens to us on the job. The demands of the workplace and the effects of work on our sense of identity and social status make it that much harder to stand outside the shadow of self.

Philosopher and curmudgeon Bertrand Russell once quipped that there were only two kinds of work: "First, altering the position of matter at or near the earth's surface relative to other matter; second, telling other people to do so. The first kind is unpleasant and ill-paid; the second is pleasant and highly paid." Russell went on to suggest that he and the vast majority of humankind, of course, prefer the second. That is, if we must work, most of us would prefer management versus labor, mental versus manual, rank versus file.

More conventionally, a lot of us simply define work as that which we get paid to do—and it may be something we would not choose to do if we weren't paid to do it. As newspaper columnist Mike Royko once said, "If work is so good, how come they have to pay us to do it?" This correlation of trading labor for dollars as a defining principle of work holds true for college professors, cement finishers, senators, and hit men alike. But perhaps in its most general and benign sense, work can be best defined as any activity we need to do (show up at the office every day) or want to do (paint the garage, plant tulip bulbs, or write a poem for a poetry slam) to achieve the basic requirements of life or to maintain a certain lifestyle. Work, then, is that which we are compelled to do out of need or desire: the need for money and the desire for self-expression and personal accomplishment. The question of which of these compulsions is greatest and who has which is another issue entirely. Work remains what we have to do. Only if we're lucky will it be pleasant, well paid, and cause for happiness. The degree to which we find this combination is the degree to which work, any work, is satisfying.

No matter what the particulars of the work, there is at least one issue that blue- and white-collar workers have in common—long hours on the job. The philosopher Josef Pieper said that "we are fettered to the process of work." Translation: We are captives of our jobs; we are consumed and time bound by what we do. You don't have to be a scholar or a sage to know that Pieper's right. Our lives do *seem* busier, fuller, more fatiguing than ever before. Sociologist Arlie Russell Hochschild suggests that modern workers talk about sleep deprivation in the same way that hungry people talk about food.

Economist Juliet Schor estimates that annual hours on the job, across all industries and occupations, have been increasing over the last 25 years, so that the average employee is now on the job 163 more hours than 25 years ago, or the equivalent of an extra month per year. In her 1991 best-seller, *The Overworked American*, she claimed that one-fourth of all full-time workers spent 49 or more hours on the job each week. Of these, almost half were at work 60 hours or more. Management guru Charles Handy wrote in 1994 that the typical American worked 47 hours per week, for an annual total of 2,330 hours, and he projected that in 2014 the average American worker will put in 3,000 hours per year on the job. In 1996, Thomas Geoghegan, a labor lawyer and author, estimated that middle-management types and senior executives endure a 55- to 65-hour workweek, and that 11 percent of all workers report working more than 65 hours per week. In 1997, in her important analysis on work and the family, *The Time Bind*, Hochschild reported that both men and women workers average slightly more than 47 hours a week. Finally, in a 1999 study, a Cornell University research project found that, on average, Americans work 350 hours more per year than Europeans and 70 hours more a year than the Japanese, whose language includes a word, *karoshi*, that means "death from overwork." If some of these figures and projections are accurate, by the year 2010, the average workweek could exceed 58 hours.

What has to be kept in mind, of course, is that these figures reflect only the hours on the job and do not represent the other aspects of our workday, such as getting to and from the job, and unpaid work devoted to household and family responsibilities. A 1993 survey conducted by the Families and Work Institute of New York concluded that each spouse in a double-income household with kids puts in a minimum of 15 hours a day between work, commuting, chores, and child care. These figures, based on a Monday-through-Friday schedule, mean that each spouse has already logged in 75 hours before the weekend. Moreover, although Sundays in many households are still reserved for family outings and social events, Saturdays are usually just another workday. Lists of household tasks are drawn up, chores are assigned, projects are attended to, and kids are schlepped to music lessons and the mall.

Whatever the exact amount of time each of us is putting into the job, it is both palpably and statistically clear to most of us that we are working harder and longer than ever before. And along with the extra hours, the tempo, intensity, and stresses associated with our work seem to be accelerating. We cram more and more into each day, and yet we feel that we never have enough time to do all that must be done. In a 2001 phone survey of more than a thousand households, the Families and Work Institute discovered that American families feel overworked and that they are doing too much on the job. Fifty-five percent of those surveyed reported feeling overwhelmed by how much work they have to do; 45 percent felt that they have to do many jobs at once and multitask too often; 59 percent complained that they were unable to reflect on and perfect the work they were doing; and, finally, 90 percent agreed strongly that they work "too fast," "too hard," and "that they never have enough time to get a job done properly."

According to yet another Families and Work Institute study in 1999, 63 percent of people in the United States say they want to work less, up from only 17 percent in 1994. A 1999 study conducted by NYU and the University of Pennsylvania found that "45 to 50 percent of workers (and 80 percent of those working more than 50 hours a week) said they would prefer to work fewer hours, and more than 25 percent said they would take a pay cut to make it happen." Another survey in 2000 found that even college students and recent graduates place "flexible hours" at the top of the list of the job benefits they most desire—above health insurance, vacations, and stock options. The moral of all this seems clear. Workers are united in their belief that even a good job, a great job—a job with terrific pay, perks, and prestige—can demand too much of us. Jobs can eat up too much of our time, our energy, our passion, and our inner selves. All this busyness also can hold us in bad situations far too long: it can keep us from discovering a life's work for which we are better suited. "Because work addiction keeps us busy, we stay estranged from our essential selves," writes psychologist Diane Fassel. "An aspect of that estrangement is that we cease asking ourselves if we are doing our right work. Are we actually performing the task or pursuing the vocation we need to be doing? Is it good for us, for our families, and the universe?"

"It Comes with the Territory"

> All work marks us, molds us, and gives us meaning and identity.
>
> **—Studs Terkel**

In the last scene of Arthur Miller's *Death of a Salesman*, Willy Loman's family and friends are standing at his graveside saying their goodbyes and reflecting on the character and legacy of the deceased.

Willy, they suggest, was a dreamer, a schemer, a talker and teller of tall tales, a con man constantly searching for the big score. But for all of his big talk and even bigger dreams, both his mouth and his ideas were too large for his talents and abilities. Willy, they say, was a failure. But even worse, he was the kind of failure who could never admit it, either to himself or to others. And so right up to the end, Willy went on dreaming and scheming and hoping for that one big sale to come along and set him up for life.

Only one of those gathered at Willy's grave defends him. "Nobody . . . blame this man," he says. "You don't understand: Willy was a salesman. . . . A salesman has got to dream. . . . It comes with the territory." It was Willy's job to smile, talk a lot, glad-hand one and all, says his defender. His job was to sell himself, sell his dream and his ideas, sell his product. It was his job that made him what he was.

"It comes with the territory" is now part of the lexicon. It conveys an acceptance of all parts of a job, being shaped by a job, and doing whatever you must in order to get a job done. Perhaps Willy Loman was a failure and a fool because he didn't recognize that he had neither the temperament nor the talent for his chosen profession, but being a salesman shaped him; it drew out the best and the worst in him and made him what he was. To paraphrase Winston Churchill, first we choose and shape our work, and then it shapes us—sometimes forever.

Whether we have a good job or a bad one, whether we love it or hate it, succeed in it or fail, work is at the center of our lives and influences who we are and all that we do. Where we live, how well we live, whom we see socially, what and where we consume and purchase, how we educate our children—all of these are determined in large part by the way in which we earn a living.

Our own sense of identity is also intimately tied to our work—and in ways that have little to do with the home and lifestyle that the money we make brings. Witness the way we identify ourselves when we meet strangers. Robert Kahn explores this phenomenon in his book *Work and Health*:

> When people ask that most self-identifying of questions—Who am I?—they answer in terms of their occupation: toolmaker, press operator, typist, doctor, construction worker, teacher. Even people who are not working identify themselves by their former work or their present wish for it, describing themselves as retired or unemployed. And work that is not paid lacks significance, much as we might wish it otherwise. Many people who are usefully occupied, but not paid, respond to questions in ways that deprecate both their activities and themselves. A women who takes care of a home and several children and is engaged in a wide range of community activities may answer with that tired and inaccurate phrase, "just a housewife." A retired man equally busy with an assortment of projects, is likely to say, "Oh, I'm retired; I don't do anything."

So work is not just about earning a livelihood. It is not just about getting paid, about gainful employment. Nor is it only about the use of one's mind and body to accomplish a specific task or project. Work is also one of the most significant contributing factors to one's inner life and development. Beyond mere survival, we create ourselves in our work. In his classic article, "Work and the Self," Everett C. Hughes argued that work is fundamental to the development of personality. Because work preoccupies our lives and is the central focus of our time and energies, it not only provides us with an income, it literally names us, identifies us, to both ourselves and others. Hughes was convinced that even when we are dissatisfied with or dislike the work that we do, choice of occupation irrevocably "labels" us, and he contended that we cannot fully understand a person unless we understand his or her work and how he or she deals with it.

In the long run, work can prove to be a boon or a burden, creative or crippling, a means to personal happiness or a prescription for despair. But no matter where we wind up on this spectrum, where we work, how we work, what we do at work, and the general climate and culture of the workplace indelibly mark us for life. Work is the means by which we form our character and complete ourselves as persons. We literally create ourselves in our work. To restate the old Italian proverb *tu sei quello che mangi* (you are what you eat) in regard to work, *tu sei quello che fai* (you are the work you do). Work is a necessary and defining activity in the development of the adult personality.

A few years ago, I attended a family wedding, and the first person I saw was my Uncle Frank. (He was not really my blood uncle. He was a friend of the family and a contemporary of my father. As a sign of respect, I always called him

Zio [uncle].) "Hey, college kid," he said to me as he shook
my hand in a viselike grip and peppered my shoulder with
a series of heavy blows. "How you been?" Uncle Frank
was in his mid-seventies, but his punches still hurt, as did
his annoying habit of calling me "college kid." I had just
turned 55. "Uncle Frank," I said, massaging my shoulder,
"you look great. Where did you get the tan? Have you
been playing a lot of golf?" "Naw," he said, "you know
I hate golf. I had a couple of jobs this month." "Jobs?
But you've been retired for ten years!" "Yeah, but they
were easy jobs," said Uncle Frank. "A couple of drive-
ways, some concrete steps, a few sidewalks. It was a piece
of cake." "Uncle Frank," I said, "this doesn't make sense.
Is something wrong? Do you need money?" "No! No!"
said Uncle Frank. "It's nothing like that." "Then why?"
I persisted. "Why did you take these jobs?" He smiled,
grabbed me roughly, and drew me to him. "Because," he said
with a wink, "I wanted to see if I could still do it, college kid.
Capisce? I just wanted to see if I could still do it."

According to theologian Gregory Baum, "labor is the axis
of human self-making." We both establish and recognize ourselves in our work. Work allows us to find out what we can and
cannot do, how we are seen by others, and how we see ourselves. In work, we discover our boundaries and limits as well

as our capacities for success. Work is the yardstick by which we measure ourselves against others. It is the means by which we establish our rank, role, and function within a community. Work not only conditions our lives; it is a necessary condition for life. Men have always known this and have accepted it as part of their lot. As one 45-year-old machinist put it, "Being a man means being willing to put all your waking hours into working to support your family. If you ask for [too much] time off, or if you turn down overtime, it means you're lazy or you're a wimp." As more and more women have entered the workplace, they too have been forced to confront this fundamental truth of adult existence: Not having a job means you're a person without salary, stuff, or status.

Assuredly other factors enter into the equation of self-identity; for example, genetic inheritance, race, gender, ethnicity, sexual orientation, religious training, and family background. But even with all of these, work remains an irreducible given, the most common experience of adult life. The lessons we learn at work help formulate who we become and what we value as individuals and as a society. Whatever the conditions of our labor, work shapes us and, unfortunately, often malforms us. But for good or ill, work makes us human because we make something of ourselves through work, and in so doing we recognize ourselves and others. And yet, as E. F. Schumacher has indicated, despite the centrality of work in human life, the question "What does the work do to the worker?" is seldom asked. Workers and scholars alike regularly debate the benefits as well as the drawbacks of particular jobs in specific industries, but only rarely do they address the overall effect of work on the psyche and moral character of the worker.

Movie director Elia Kazan said that the one absolute lesson he had learned in life is that "a man is what he does," and, consequently, that the secret to a good life is to make a living at what you want to do. As sociologist Douglas La Bier asserted, careers and identities are inextricably tied up; indeed, they are equivalent. People are what they do, and what people do affects every aspect of who they are. The lessons we learn in our work and at the workplace become the metaphors we apply to life and the means by which we digest the world. The meter and measure of work serves as our mapping device to explain and order the geography of life. We are "typed" by our work and, in turn, we analyze and evaluate the world and others by our acquired work "types." Our work circumscribes what we know, how we know, and how we select and categorize the things we choose to see, react to, or respond to. Work influences our use and our repertoire of personal and professional learned skills and behaviors. As Samuel Butler once wrote, "Every man's work, whether it be literature or music or pictures or architecture or anything else, is always a portrait of himself."

Cops know things you and I don't. It's knowledge crafted
out of years spent on the street, sizing up and dealing with the volatile, cunning, confused, comic, tragic,
often goofy behavior of human beings from every social,
economic, and mental level, and it's knowledge won as
a by-product of investigating criminal specialties such
as homicide, sex crimes, property crimes, and narcotics.
A cop who works traffic has peered deeper into the
recesses of the human psyche than most shrinks. A cop
who works homicide, or sex crimes, will tell you things
Dostoyesvsky only guessed at.

—Connie Fletcher, *What Cops Know*

Totalitarianism in the Workplace

Given the centrality of work in our lives—the sheer number
of hours we put in on the job, the money that we make
and the stuff it allows us to acquire, the kinds of status and
success we can achieve on the job—how can work not affect
our values and sense of ethics? How is it possible to retain
a private sense of objectivity, impartiality, and a respectful
concern for others? How is it possible to not be co-opted by
the needs and demands of the workplace? How is it possible
to at least be swayed, if not totally compromised, by the work
environment that sustains us?

Even in Death: Job First, Relatives Later!

OBITUARY NOTICE

"Joseph DeLucca, leading Civil-Rights attorney, dead at 72.

He is survived by his wife, Maria, and his beloved children . . . "

Work, all work, creates its own self-contained moral universe. Every job, good or bad, creates its own experiences, its own standards, its own pace, and its own self-defined *weltansschauung* (worldview). Every job, depending on the intensity, depth, and duration of the individual worker's involvement, can have either immediate or long-term effects on the worker. Analogous to psychiatrist Robert J. Lifton's understanding of "delayed stress" or "post-stress syndrome among soldiers who have engaged in combat," many of the lessons we learn on a particular job remain with us forever, consciously or subconsciously, as part of our catalog of learned experiences. Some of these experiences, according to Lifton, inform us and direct us positively, and some can haunt us and have a negative effect years later. Lifton asserts that no soldier walks away from combat untouched by the experience. The same can be said of most jobs, even those far less traumatic than soldiering. The habits we acquire on the job, what we are exposed to, what is demanded of us, and the pressure of peers *can* change, influence, and/or erode our personal conduct and standards. At the very least: When everybody else in the workplace is doing "it" (whatever "it" is), isn't it natural to at least ask yourself, "Why not me, too?"

The two individuals who most eloquently explain the phenomenon of the institutional co-option of the individual worker are Howard S. Schwartz and Robert Jackall. Schwartz, in his radical but underappreciated managerial text *Narcissistic Process and Corporate Decay*, argues that corporations and businesses are not bastions of benign, community-oriented ethical reasoning, nor can they, because of the demands and requirements of business, be models of moral behavior. The rule of business, said Schwartz, remains the survival of the fittest, and the goal of survival engenders a combative "us against them" mentality, which condones getting ahead by any means necessary. Schwartz calls this phenomenon "organizational totalitarianism." Organizations and the people who manage them create for themselves a self-contained, self-serving worldview, which rationalizes anything done on their behalf and which does not require justification on any grounds outside of themselves.

This narcissistic perspective, Schwartz suggests, imposes Draconian requirements on all participants in organizational life: do your work; achieve organizational goals; obey and exhibit loyalty to your superiors; disregard personal values and beliefs; obey the law when necessary, obfuscate it when possible; and, deny internal or external information at odds with the stated organizational worldview. Within such a "totalitarian" logic, neither leaders nor followers operate as independent agents. To maintain their place or to get ahead, all must conform.

In *Moral Mazes,* Robert Jackall parallels, from a sociological rather than a psychological perspective, much of Schwartz's analysis of organizational behavior. According to critic and commentator Thomas W. Norton, both Jackall and Schwartz seek to understand why and how organizational ethics and behavior are so often reduced to either loyalty or the simple adulation and mimicry of one's superiors. Though Schwartz argues that individuals are captives of the impersonal structural logic of organizational totalitarianism, Jackall contends that out of necessity "organizational actors become personally loyal to their superiors, always seeking their approval and are committed to them as persons rather than as representatives of the abstractions of organizational authority." In Scott Adams' (the creator of *Dilbert*) terms, employees are forced to "suck up" to their bosses. All three authors agree that workers are prisoners of the systems they serve.

According to Jackall, organizations are examples of "patrimonial bureaucracies" wherein "fealty relations of personal loyalty" are the rule of organizational life. Jackall argued that all corporations are like fiefdoms of the Middle Ages, wherein the lord of the manor (CEO or president) offers protection, prestige, and status to his vassals (managers) and serfs (workers) in return for homage (commitment) and service (work). In such a system, says Jackall, advancement and promotion are predicated on loyalty, trust, politics, and personality at least as much as on experience, education, ability, and accomplishments. The central concern of the worker minion is to be known as the "can-do" employee, a "team player," being at the right place at the right time and "master of all the social rules." That's why in the corporate world, says Jackall, a thousand "attaboys" are wiped away with one "oh, shit!"

As in a feudal system, Jackall maintains that employees of a corporation are expected to become supporters of the status quo. Their loyalty is to the powers that be, their duty is to perpetuate performance and profit, and their values can be none other than those sanctioned by the organization. Jackall contends that the logic of every organization and the collective personality of the workplace conspire to override the desires and aspirations of the individual worker. No matter what a person believes off the job, on the job all of us are required to some extent to suspend, bracket, or only selectively manifest our personal convictions.

In Jackall's analysis, the primary imperative of every organization is to succeed. This goal of performance, which he refers to as "institutional logic," leads to the creation of a private moral universe that, by definition, is self-sustained, self-defined, and self-centered. Within such an environment, truth is socially defined, and moral behavior is determined solely by organization needs. The key virtues, for all, become the virtues of the organization: goal preoccupation, problem solving, survival or success, and, most important, playing by the "house rules." In time, says

Jackall, those initiated and invested in the system come to believe that they live in a self-contained world that is above outside critique and evaluation.

> It is difficult to be a good person in a society that is itself not good. People, after all, live and learn through the institutions of society—family, school, church, community, and the workplace—and these institutions must support the positive development of individuals if society is to produce succeeding generations of positive individuals.
>
> **—Kathleen McCourt, social theorist**

We are all workers, and although I do not want to exonerate any of us, I do have a modicum of sympathy for those individuals who find themselves compromised by the system. "Bending if not breaking the rules," "looking the other way," "closing one's eyes to the obvious," "going along to get along"—all of these tactics may be less an instance of personal choice and narcissism and much more about need and necessity based on self-preservation and survival. Fear of losing our sinecure can sometimes make cowards and fools of us all; at the very least, it can lead to laxity, mediocrity, and the anesthetization of critical thinking. Rather than standing out, being different, the fear of not being able to earn a living co-opts us, and, to use Herbert Marcuse's terminology, makes us moral slaves to the system that sustains us!

Perhaps René Descartes is wrong. Perhaps it isn't *cogito, ergo sum* ("I think, therefore I am"), but rather *labora, ergo sum* ("I work, therefore I am"). We need work, and as adults we find identity in and are identified by the work we do. Our work tells us who we are. If this is true, then we must be very careful about what we choose to do for a living, for what we do is what we become, what we believe in, and what we value.

8. Leisure and Play

Genuine leisure is a much underrated activity in America. The Puritan heritage, having escaped the controlling reins of religion, has invaded almost every other aspect of life.

—**John Sullivan,** *Chicago Sun Times*

The correlative component of how work influences our moral decision making is the importance of play and leisure in the formation of our ethical standards and our ability to stand outside of the shadow of self. Just as our work boxes us in, delimits our options, and forces moral compromise, so too our lack of sufficient rest, leisure, and play enervates us, erodes critical reflection, and impedes our ability to make ethical decisions.

Long hours on the job, the frenzy of multitasking, the drudgery of household chores, and the responsibility of children leave too many of us with too little time for leisure, play, and recuperation. We are both an overworked and under-rested society, and rest is a critical component for both physical and psychological well-being.

In a 1995 cover story, *Newsweek* reported that 25 percent of us say we're fried by our work, frazzled by the lack of time, and exhausted by life in general. Symptoms of exhaustion and fatigue are now among the top five reasons people consult with their doctors. Although physicians are quick to point out that "exhaustion" is an umbrella term and not a medical term or a diagnosis, fatigue symptoms can herald any number of serious illnesses. (However, chronic fatigue syndrome, also called Epstein-Barr and yuppie flu, is very rare, affecting only 5 percent of those who suffer long-term fatigue). Dr. Sheldon Miller, chairman of the psychology department at Northwestern University, says that exhaustion is the body crying out, "I've had it."

According to a survey conducted in 2001 by the National Sleep Foundation, our workaholic lifestyle is turning America into a "nodding-off nation," with 40 percent of those surveyed reporting difficulties staying awake during the day and on the job. The poll reported that although people need between seven and ten hours of sleep each night, 62 percent of those surveyed sleep less than eight hours per night, and of those, 31 percent reported sleeping seven hours, and 31 percent sleep six hours or less per night. Thirty-eight percent of all those surveyed said they sleep less now than they did five years ago and suffer from mild to chronic bouts of insomnia and sleep apnea. Maybe all of this helps to explain the phenomenal success of Starbucks. Maybe the real secret to their success isn't so much the quality of their coffee as it is our need for caffeine, and our need to stay awake!

If you're like most people, you know that a sleepless night can zap your energy and turn your brain to mush. Well, says Eve Van Cauter, professor of medicine and sleep research at the University of Chicago, that's just the beginning of your problems when you chronically miss too much sleep. Because sleep serves so many purposes. According to Dr. Van Cauter, not getting enough sleep appears to have wide-ranging effects on our health. "We need sleep for almost everything," says Van Cauter. "Studies are beginning to show that no matter what system you look at—whether it's memory, learning, decision making, the immune system, endocrine system, or sugar metabolism—when you look at those systems in subjects who are sleep derived on a chronic basis, you find exaggerated negative effects." Sleep researchers are now in general agreement that chronic lack of sleep may be as bad for a person's health as smoking, a poor diet, and a lack of exercise. We need sleep, says Van Cauter, to rest and build our brains, to heal, to clear our cobwebs, to slow aging and dementia, and to help avoid obesity, diabetes, and hypertension.

> My father taught me to work, but not to love it. I never did like to work, and I don't deny it. I'd rather read, tell stories, crack jokes, talk, laugh—anything but work.
>
> **—Abraham Lincoln**

All Work and No Play

My thesis here is a simple one. When our lives are too hectic, when we don't rest and play enough, we make bad decisions and life choices. Exhaustion and stress lead to a loss of focus, a diminished capacity for careful consideration, and the inability to maintain objectivity and perspective. To get a better handle on this overall phenomenon, let's define a few basic collateral terms.

LAZY

Wayne E. Oates, psychologist, pastoral counselor, and the originator of the term "workaholic," argues that as a culture we are steadfastly of two minds about our understanding of the term "lazy." On the one hand, in our workaday world of intense competition, productivity, and status seeking, to be called lazy is to be despised by others and often by ourselves as well. "Lazy" is often used as a "four-letter word" to ridicule individuals who lack energy and effort, or who are slow moving, sluggish, slothful, or just plain goofing off. To be labeled with the moniker of lazy is to be thought of as immature, undependable, irresponsible, indolent, and/or uselessly idle.

On the other hand, says Oates, we long to be lazy, to do nothing, to be purposely inactive. We crave lazy summer afternoons. We brag about lazy winter weekends, or at the very least, the luxury of "long lazy Sunday mornings with the *New York Times*." In one sense, says Oates, we see being lazy as a status symbol, a badge of honor, a privilege and a right we have earned by our labors. To be rightfully idle, to be righteously lazy, purposeless, with no tasks to do is a direct reflection of our success at work. To openly rest, relax, recuperate, to *redux* (to recover, return to health) without worrying about what others might think is a testimony to our success and status as workers. After all, besides being judged by what we do, how much we earn, where we live, and what we own, we are judged by our "acquired time off the job."

RECREATION

Even though we don't do it enough, we all seek to be idle, to be lazy, to enjoy rest as a natural antidote to the fatigue and frustrations of the job. When asked what he would do after retirement, Justice Thurgood Marshall of the U.S. Supreme Court answered, "Sit on my rear end!" But even well-practiced lassitude has its limits. No one can remain idle forever, except possibly teenagers. After a while, even the benefits of laziness can become a burden or at the very least lead to boredom and the kind of anxiety that results from being excessively idle. All of us naturally seek some form of diversion or recreation—activities that change the pace, the place, or the nature of our usual habits, activities that we enjoy or that relieve stress. In common parlance, this is what most of us mean by the term "play."

Unfortunately, for too many of us, our various forms of recreation and play are really about rehabilitation, recuperation, and recovery rather than rapture and the possibility of the rediscovery of self. For many of us, our diversions or play are really only momentary distractions from the usual pace of life. They are designed to overcome fatigue, numb awareness, or appease a particular appetite—all for the purpose of reinvigorating and restoring us to the work task at hand. In other words, a lot of what we do, how we spend our time off the job—hobbies, clubs, organizations, films, theater, music, workouts, friends, TV, whatever—is really about taking a break, filling in time, catching up, recharging our batteries, overcoming our fatigue and feelings of stupefaction so that we go back to the job to endure and earn more.

Leisure

Because too many of us live in a world of total work, we think that leisure is at least minimally achieved by the mere absence of work. Because we are so eager to escape the burdens of work, we think that any form of nonwork, quiet time, down time constitutes some form of rest, recreation, and/or leisure. Well, we're wrong. To be idle, to be without a task, to be doing nothing are necessary but not sufficient conditions for the achievement of genuine leisure.

G. K. Chesterton, English essayist, editor, critic, novelist, lecturer, broadcaster—and, ironically, a card-carrying workaholic—spent a great deal of time and energy writing about the exact nature and necessity of leisure. Chesterton argues that leisure is about "free time," "time which one can spend as one pleases." The root of the word "leisure" comes from the Latin *licere*, which means "to be permitted," suggesting that leisure is about unstructured, free-choice time. But, says Chesterton, there are wiser and lesser choices one can make in regard to one's free time. Leisure, he said, can be used to describe three different sorts of things. "The first (and the most common form of leisure) is being allowed to do something (something other than work). The second is being allowed to do anything (anything that engages your interest or desires). And the third is being allowed to do nothing (a noble habit that is both difficult and rare)."

For Chesterton the "noble habit of doing nothing" means to do no practical, utilitarian, or quotidian task. He does not mean that leisure is equal to inertia or to do nothing at all. Rather, leisure is the opportunity to do other than that which is necessary or required. To do as one pleases. To be freed from the mundane. To be free to pursue the unusual, the inexplicable, the irrelevant, the interesting, and the idiosyncratic.

VACATION

In Latin the word for vacation is *vacare*, "to be empty, non-occupied," "to suspend activity," "to do nothing." Work represents the everyday routine, and vacations are temporary interruptions. On vacations we turn aside, go in the opposite direction, vacate ourselves from our usual course or purpose. Vacations connote downtime, choice, freedom, personal discretion, and activities an individual engages in for his or her own purposes and pleasures.

Vacations are seen as an antidote to work. They are medicine, a remedy for counteracting the effects of labor. Oates believes that vacations offer us an opportunity to "empty ourselves of our multiple roles in life." Vacations allow us to be away from the job, to change the patterns of our day, to alter our routine, to reconfigure our actions and habits, to rediscover ourselves.

"Sadly," says Joe Robinson, former editor of the now defunct adventure-travel magazine *Escape* (apparently no one had time to read it!), "we're the most vacation-starved nation in the world." In this society, says Robinson, we perversely allow "downtime for machinery and maintenance and repair, but we don't allow it for employees." America's most hazardous work-related illness, says Robinson, is VD—that is, "vacation deficit disorder" or "vacation starvation." There is only one other country with fewer vacation days than America (10–13) and that is Mexico (6). And what is worse is that in America these vacation days are not required by law, but rather are the result of negotiated contracts or custom and tradition. In comparison to the mandated vacation schedules of other industrialized nations, says Robinson, American workers are suffering from a serious leisure lag: Italy, 42 days; Germany, 35; Sweden, 32; Spain, 30; Denmark, 30; Ireland, 28. Even the work-addicted Japanese get 25 mandated vacation days a year.

Although the concept of vacation is part of our general cultural expectations, it is not a reality in the life of every worker. According to a 2001 report by the American Family Institute of New York, one quarter of the American workforce does not take a regular vacation; two-thirds of people who earn $10,000 or less a year take less than one week off per year; and day workers, who regularly experience "enforced time off" (not hired for the day), take zero planned vacation days off. And let's not forget George Will's assertion that even while on vacation 40 percent of working Americans remain in "daily contact with their offices, by e-mail, from their cabins, by cell-phones from their canoes."

Vacations, long walks, quiet weekends, down time, time alone, time to think should not be considered a perk or a privilege but rather a necessity of the human condition. We need to not always be doing. We must studiously do less in order to be more.

The Need to Do Nothing at All

Because our cultural mythology is steeped in the hard work and accomplishment of our pioneering forbearers, we just *don't do nothing well!* We are not known as a nation of relaxers! Despite the competing mythology of the 1960s, we are not a laid-back nation. We rarely deliberately devote ourselves to idleness. Although I know it sounds like a Zen paradox, we almost never slow down enough to experience the experience of *not doing anything at all*. We rarely attune our inner ear to the needs of our inner self. We usually stay too busy. We usually do too much, and in the doing we insulate ourselves from ourselves and others.

In an almost completely forgotten book, *Solitude: A Return to the Self,* English psychiatrist Anthony Storr speaks of the profoundly neglected human need for solitude. Storr notes that the state of solitude is about calmness, centeredness, and focus. It's the ability to get "lost in the present." It's about being able to rivet our attention, getting in touch with our deepest thoughts and feelings. It's about being able to ruminate without distraction, to meditate, to idly muse, to become totally absorbed in thought.

One of the many paradoxes of the human condition is that although we need each other and learn from each other, we are also distracted by the presence of others and kept from ourselves by others. Greta Garbo was psychologically profound and not just being "campy" when she demanded her right to privacy: "I want to be alone." All of us need to be alone. Solitude acts as our gyroscope and compass. We founder or travel less well without it. Solitude, says Storr, allows us a respite from the distractions and distortions of the everyday world. Solitude gives us access to our own thoughts. It is a form of self-therapy. It allows us to hear ourselves think. It allows us to think out loud to ourselves. To paraphrase e. e. cummings, How do I know what I really think, until I get a chance to hear what I have to say?

Of course, achieving solitude is easier said than done. As William James pointed out, reality is a "booming, buzzing, confusion." The excessive busyness of our multitasked lives and the constant overload of outside stimuli are much more conducive to the production of migraines than the pursuit of meaning. Nevertheless, suggests Storr, "finding down-time," "time outside of usual time," "time to reflect on time," is a *sine qua non* condition for emotional and intellectual stability. For Storr, part of our emotional, ethical, and intellectual maturity is measured by our ability to achieve and cope with solitude. Solitude, says Storr, is linked to self-discovery and self-realization. It is both the catalyst and conduit for change and creativity. Storr believes that no one will ever fully develop the capacities of their intellect without the solemnity and intellectual sanctuary provided by solitude.

Theologian Wayne Muller, in his insightful and moving text *Sabbath*, argues that in the relentless busyness of modern life, we have lost the rhythm between work and rest. And because we do not rest enough, says Muller, we lose our way, and are often unsure about how to proceed. Although the Sabbath is a specific religious practice, the concept of Sabbath, says Muller, is also a larger metaphor, a starting point to invoke a conversation about the necessity of rest. Like solitude, Sabbath is a way of creating a time when we can examine who we are, what we know, and reflect on what we have. Sabbath, like solitude, is about letting go, being fallow, and looking within.

Given the pressures of work and the blitzkrieg pace of our lives off the job, too many details get overlooked, too many niceties get lost in the shuffle, and too many standards and values are compromised by the demands of the moment. Here's the problem. When life is an Olympic endurance event ("The Everydayathon"), when are we supposed to have fun? When do we have an opportunity to think clearly? When will there be time to be human? Some things simply cannot and should not be done going full speed—like love, sex, conversation, contemplation, family, food, and friends. The bottom line seems clear: Fatigue and the frenzy of overstimulation can block objectivity, delimit perspective, and often deaden our ability to calculate and evaluate logically.

Without true leisure and the chance to rest, dream, and wonder, we are diminished as individuals and a society. And without leisure, rest, and play, we too often simply endure life rather than enjoy it.

In Chinese, the pictography for the word "busy" is composed of two characters, heart and killing. Hmm! Interesting, don't you agree?

Anna Quindlen is right, "doing nothing is something." For Quindlen we create our public identity in the work that we do, but it is in our "non-work-time," our "downtime" that we create and become our true selves. To paraphrase the words of Josef Pieper, leisure is not only the basis of culture, leisure is the basis of our ethical selves.

> Every now and then go away and have a little relaxation.
>
> To remain constantly at work will diminish your judgement.
>
> Go some distance away, because work (and life) will be in
>
> perspective and a lack of harmony is more readily seen.
>
> **—Leonardo da Vinci**

9. Leadership, Money, Power

The competitive urge is a fine, wholesome direction of energy. But . . . the desire to win must be wedded to an ideal, an ethical way of life. It must never become so strong that it dwarfs every other aspect of the game of life.

—Edward R. Murrow, CBS correspondent

The quest for riches darkens the sense of right and wrong.

—Antiphanes (c. 388–c. 311 B.C.)

I have been teaching business ethics as a required course to the uninterested and the unwilling for more years than I care to admit in print. Each semester, for the first few weeks of class, the students sit there mutely, staring at me, daring me, challenging me with their eyes to convince them that this course will be worth their time and effort. Their contemptuous facial expressions seem to be radiating the same silent message: "Come on, ethics in our private lives is hard enough, but business ethics—you've got to be kidding! Business ethics is not just a contradiction in terms, an oxymoron! It's a null set! It's a lie! Read the papers, Doc!

Business is about status, stuff, and success. So you take risks, you bend the rules a little, and yeah, sometimes, you get caught. But if you want to get ahead, that's the way the game is played."

Top Ten Oxymorons

10. Painless Dentistry

9. Military Intelligence

8. Jumbo Shrimp

7. Legally Drunk

6. City Workers

5. Rap Music

4. Working Vacations

3. Airline Food

2. Equitable Divorce Settlement

1. Pleasant and Cooperative Teenager

Believe me, I've heard it all, and not just from students. Family and friends have not been above taking cheap shots at me as well. My son once asked me, "Gee, Dad, isn't lecturing about business ethics like trying to nail Jell-O to the wall?" And a longtime handball partner and *former* friend once said, "Do you really teach business ethics? My goodness, after the first ten minutes of your first class, what do you do with the rest of the semester?" Clearly, one is rarely a prophet in one's own home!

And yet, at one level I do understand their collective cynicism and glibness. Their comments are not just cavalier and without some merit and creditability. They're right, check the news media. What Fortune 1000 firms made the headlines today for misappropriation of funds? And what famous CEO is on national TV doing the "perp-walk" in front of a federal courthouse? Ethics is hard to define, and business ethics is even harder. Perhaps, like pornography, we only recognize business ethics when we see it. The problem is, we so rarely see it!

In this society, we have made a fetish out of being ambitious and achieving financial success. Competition and rugged individualism are part of our collective myth and mantra. Looking out for one's own best interest has become a way of life even though it regularly means that others may get stepped on in the process. Astonishingly, the notion that such behavior might be destructive to others as well as debasing to ourselves is rarely raised, let alone seriously considered. Seemingly we live in a society in which ethical laissez-faire has been elevated to a national credo. As a consequence, it has become terribly easy to lose our way. And the only time we have to apologize for our misdeeds or the misfortune we cause others is if and when we get caught.

I think that too many of us believe that the stakes and standards involved in business are simply different from, more important than, and, perhaps, even antithetical to the principles and practices of ethics. Ethics is something we may preach and practice at home in our private lives, but not in business. After all, it could cost us prestige, position, profits, and success. Just as it is difficult in our personal lives to keep our narcissism in check, the task is made that much more difficult in our professional lives when cash, comfort, and sinecure are on the line.

Scams: The Big Ones

Behind every great fortune lies a crime.

—**Honore de Balzac**

Even though I have argued that change is real, sometimes even when things appear to change, they wind up coming back again. The players may change, particulars may change, but the underlying principles and issues can and very often do repeat themselves. Similar kinds of situations and events regularly insinuate themselves into our collective time-space continuum. And as George Santayana has so famously warned us, "Those who cannot remember the past are condemned to repeat it."

In the field of business ethics, it doesn't require encyclopedic knowledge or a huge leap of imagination to come up with examples that substantiate Santayana's thesis. In the 1920s there was Charles Ponzi's "postal coupon scam," which in the 1970s reappeared as Robert Vesco's "mutual funds scam," which appeared yet again in the 1980s with Charles Keating in his "security fraud scam" in the savings and loan industry. Then there's Ivan Boesky in the 1980s, and the charges of "insider trading" that were recently leveled against America's favorite doyenne of domesticity, Martha Stewart. Although these charges were dismissed by the judge, Ms. Stewart was convicted on March 5, 2004, of lying, conspiracy, and obstruction of justice. Also, let's not forget the "junk bond" king Michael Milken and his pushing the limits of financial risk taking, and the more contemporary brand of "cowboy capitalism" practiced by a number of now-nonexistent dot-com enterprises. And lest we forget, there's the Ford cover-up of the Pinto's exploding gas tank, and more recent headlines decrying the accident rates of Ford Explorers.

Of course, the most famous example of recent corporate perfidy and failure is Enron and the now-defunct "white-shoed accounting firm," Arthur Andersen. To its dismay, Enron has become an icon of an era. It has become the poster child for corporate mismanagement, a metaphor for corporate corruption, and shorthand for corporate greed. Its name has become a term of derision and disdain and has spawned a new lexicon for business chicanery and failure. You can now be "*Enron* people," "be *Enronish* to others," "practice *Enronomics*," "see *Enronish* sights," or "experience a failure of *Enronian* proportions." The name is also used as an umbrella term for the cadre of other corporate giants who found themselves in the public spotlight for legal and ethical failures: Tyco, WorldCom, Global Crossing, Adelphia, ImClone, Boeing, Hollinger International, Health South, and the new international scandal—Italy's Parmalat.

What happened at Enron combines all of the elements, which makes it a perfect case study in business ethics—or the lack thereof. But at the core of Enron's failure and failings remains the issue that is central to both individual and organizational behavior: the inability to stand outside of the shadow of self.

The obvious question is, of course, how did Enron transform itself from one of America's paragons to one of its chief pariahs? How can it be that Enron could declare bankruptcy and disillusionment overnight? How can it be that the sixth-largest energy corporation in the world winded up being vilified in the press as running a "Ponzi-watts" scheme on its customers and stockholders?

Clearly, Enron's conduct, like that of Arthur Andersen, wasn't the result of a simple lack of ethical rules and legal guidelines and requirements. Quite the contrary. The accounting profession claims the second-oldest code of ethical standards in existence (second to the medical profession's Hippocratic Oath). The American Institute of Certified Public Accountants (AICPA), claims that its Code of Professional Conduct applies to all CPAs in both the public and private sectors. The AICPA also requires that CPAs take continuing education courses in accounting policy and ethics in order to remain certified practitioners.

Arthur Levitt, former chairman of the Securities and Exchange Commission, has argued that the stock market, accounting industry, and financial industries may be the most regulated businesses in American commerce. In his new book *Take on The Street*, Levitt argues that "rules, regulations, requirements, and guidelines exist in abundance" and should be able to do the job. But, says Levitt, they are unable to do so because of a "web of dysfunctional relationships among analysts, brokers, and corporations" who are out to beat the system. Business ethicist John Dobson totally agrees with Levitt's analysis. "Ethical guidelines," says Dobson, "are viewed in the same way as legal or accounting rules: they are constraints to be, wherever possible, circumvented or just plain ignored in the pursuit of self-interest, or in the pursuit of the misconceived interests of the organization."

Perhaps the most obvious and the simplest answer to Enron's behavior is that "it was all about the money." This is, by no means, a novel thesis. Money, greed, the pursuit of excess profits, power, and stuff have always been part of the human repertoire of options. As Alan Greenspan has pointed out, "It is not that humans have become any more greedy than in generations past. . . . It is that the venues to express greed have grown enormously."

It's important to keep in mind that Enron achieved its success in the midst of the boom days and market euphoria of the Clinton administration. Everyone expected to make money. Everyone was making money. Enron was making more money than anyone. And apparently, although the full extent of Enron's collective as well as individual employee culpability is yet to be fully determined, many of the folks at Enron seemed to be willing to do almost anything to keep the revenue flow growing. As one National Public Radio commentator put it, "Behind the slick exterior of being a modern, cutting edge, money-making corporate giant, Enron made money the old fashioned way—it stole it from us! In the end, the only difference between Enron and depression-era bank robbers, was that the bank robbers used guns and masks during their stick-ups."

> "A business that makes nothing but money is a poor kind of business."
>
> **—Henry Ford**

Connected to the issue of greed, of course, is the challenge of the game itself. Clearly, a lot of the players at Enron were willing to push some of Michael Milken's theories and practices on "cowboy capitalism" to the furthest limits of logic and accountability. The former CFO of Enron, Andrew Fastow, allegedly combined many of Milken's techniques along with deceit, circumvention of the rules (by changing or suspending them), and outright thievery to achieve his objectives. Fastow has been indicted for mismanaging, misappropriating, and embezzling an estimated $390 million. On January 14, 2004, Mr. Fastow pleaded guilty to two wide-ranging conspiracy charges contained in the 98-count criminal indictment that he faced. He was sentenced to ten years in prison and was fined $29 million. The other 96 charges will be dropped only after Fastow's continued cooperation with the prosecution. On February 20, 2004, former CEO Jeffery Skilling was charged with twenty counts of securities fraud, four counts of wire fraud, ten counts of insider trading, and one count of conspiracy to commit securities and wire fraud. If convicted, Skilling faces more than $66 million in forfeitures, up to 325 years in prison, and hundreds of millions in fines. Finally, on July 7, 2004, Kenneth Lay, founder and former CEO of Enron, was indicted on 11 counts, including conspiracy to commit fraud. In a sweeping 65-page indictment, federal prosecutors cast Lay as a key player in the massive fraud that brought down Enron. The government claims that although Skilling and Fastow "spearheaded the scheme" to defraud the company, Lay was not an innocent victim and out of the loop. In fact, the government charges that at a certain point Lay "took over leadership of the conspiracy."

The first question that begs to be asked is Why? Why would someone making millions of dollars a year risk his sinecure for more? I think the answer is altogether very, very human but not altogether rational. It's about the thrill of the game—the excitement of the risk, the emotion and intellectual pleasure of the challenge. It's about the need to win, no matter what the odds. It's about the palpable rush of knowingly breaking the rules. It's about narcissistic illusions of invincibility. It's about feeling smugly superior to those who don't take chances. And every time you get away with one, it's about the arrogant certainty of one's infallibility. The second question that begs to be answered, especially in Fastow's case, is Why did he take so much? What was Fastow hoping to do with all that money? Did he think he would eventually be able to spend it? Did he think that in time he could drop $10 million, $20 million, $50 million on this or that without drawing attention to himself? (The same can be said of Dennis Kozlowski of Tyco. Didn't he think that his lavish spending habits and flamboyant lifestyle would draw attention to his conduct and raise questions about his propriety and character?) And even if Fastow just wanted to play the game but never spend the money, how is it that he didn't realize he was breaking Tony Soprano's basic rule of thievery and embezzlement: "Don't take too much. They'll notice! That's how you get caught!"?

For Enron and its fellow partners in crime, all of these issues are a piece of the puzzle. Each, it can be argued, contributed, to a greater or lesser extent, to Enron's demise and disillusionment. However, I want to contend that hubris, money, greed, arrogance, and reckless cowboy capitalism are really symptoms or, at best, only partial causes for Enron's immoral and illegal pursuit of self-destruction.

Ultimately, Enron's failure is really a result of a total breakdown of corporate structure and corporate culture brought about by the failure of corporate leadership. I am convinced that without committed ethical leadership, ethical standards will not be established, maintained, and retained in the life of any organization. The ethics of leadership affects the ethics of the workplace and helps to form the ethical choices and decisions of the workers in the workplace. Leaders set the pace by communicating ethical standards and establishing the overall vision, mission, and tone of an organization's day-to-day mundane reality.

Although complex and convoluted at the operational level, theoretically the bottom line is easy to state: The leaders of an organization, whether good or bad, ethical or unethical, create, and to a large extent control, the culture, character, and choices of that organization. As Robert Jackall has pointed out, "What is right in the corporation is not what is right in a (person's) home or . . . church. What is right in the corporation is what the guy above you wants from you."

At Enron, WorldCom, Tyco, and other corporations, the leaders created a culture that pushed the envelope, encouraging and rewarding excessive risk taking, and fixating on the bottom line without regard to ethics. In such a milieu, conflicts between organizational imperatives and external social requirements and restrictions are easy to resolve. In the words of Michael Hoffman, director of Bentley College's Center for Business Ethics, "Culture always trumps compliance!"

I believe that the central problem of ethics in business today is not a lack of awareness or a lack of moral imagination or moral reasoning, but rather the absence of moral leadership and the neglected development of a moral culture. As ethics consultant

Mike Lambert has so eloquently put it, "Ethics is not just a class you teach or a box you check, it is a way of being. It has to be something cultural."

So Whom Do We Trust?

A fish rots from the head.

—**Russian proverb**

Philosopher and leadership scholar Joanne Ciulla has argued that critical thinking and moral thinking are fundamental competences of leadership. What she is suggesting is that by job description, leaders must embrace the Socratic dictum that "an unexamined life is not worth living." That is, leaders should know how to think, know what they think, and know what they value.

All leadership is value and vision laden. All leadership, whether right or wrong, good or bad, defensible or reprehensible, is moral leadership. To phrase it more accurately, all leadership is ideologically driven or motivated by a certain philosophical perspective, series of ideas, beliefs, or values which, upon evaluation, may or may not prove to be moral in a more colloquial or normative sense. In other words, all leadership claims a particular point of view or philosophical package of ideas it wishes to advocate and advance. All forms of leadership try to establish the guidelines, set the tone, and control the manners, mores, and morals of the organization of which they are a part. There are, of course, some exceptions to my claim that the ethics of an organization is primarily dependent on leadership. For example, ethical ideas, standards, and values can and may originate anywhere within the structure of an organization. However, without the backing, encouragement, and support of the leaders of the organization, the best of intentions and ideas will wither on the vine and not become part of the ethos and culture of the organization.

When business ethicists speak of moral leadership in business, their normative standards, demands, and expectations are neither unusual nor extraordinary. Both business ethics and classical (traditional) ethics seek to respond to the demands of the "examined life." All of ethics begins with the recognition that we are not alone and are not the center of the universe. It begins when we realize that we are by nature communal creatures and that our collective existence requires us to continually make choices about what we ought to do in regard to others. Business ethics, like all of ethics, is nothing more than the study of our web of relationships with others. It is the attempt to work out the rights and obligations we have and share with others.

For business ethicists, the moral questions facing a person are age-old, and these are essentially the same issues facing business—only writ in large script. The assertion that "business is business" and that "ethics is what we try to do in our private lives" simply does not hold up to close scrutiny. Life, labor, and business are all of a piece. They are not separate games played by separate rules. As Ed Freeman, an ethicist as the Darden

Graduate School of Business at the University of Virgina, has reminded us, ethics is how we treat people face to face, person to person, day in and day out over a prolonged period of time. And business ethics, says Freeman, is how we treat people face to face, person to person, day in and day out, on the job—the people we work with, work for, and come to work to serve.

For business ethicists, the moral culture of any business is directly connected to the quality and ethical integrity of its leadership. In American philosophical circles, that means, on the one hand, the pursuit of justice, fair play, and, on the other, creating a climate of trust. Both "hands" are needed and necessary.

In 1999, Steve Samek, a managing partner of Arthur Andersen, said something that would prove to be prophetic: "The day Arthur Andersen loses the public's trust is the day we are out of business." March 14, 2002—Andersen indicted. March 15, 2002—Andersen virtually out of business. October 16, 2002—Andersen found guilty and sentenced for obstruction of justice; Andersen literally out of business—85,000 jobs lost worldwide.

Let's pause to ask a fundamental question: What exactly did Enron/Andersen do wrong? From a legal point of view, they abused, mishandled, and illegally mismanaged their statutory and fiduciary responsibilities to their stakeholders. From a philosophical point of view, the same essential answer can be given. Enron abrogated its statutory and fiduciary responsibilities to its stakeholders. Although the answer seems the same, it is and it isn't. To paraphrase the immoral words of

ground rules of business, and,
nd success. In this equation of
lores contend, the special role
must be those who establish
he art of trusting," and inspire

In Few We Trust"

:ople can be trusted?*

53%

49%

44%

39%

35%

saying yes.

hicago Tribune, **July 7, 2003**

---

nic system rests on trust. When
behavior is lax, the system is
s David Mamet in his screen-
re forced to behave in a manner
ence, prosperity, and propriety:
th anyone, assume you're in an
at they are out to cheat you."

President William J. Clinton, it all depends on what you mean by the word "fiduciary." In business circles, "fiduciary" is used as a synonym for financial obligations and duties. It is commonly understood to mean "money is owed" or that "financial obligations exist." In fact, in Latin, the root word for fiduciary is *fidĕre*, and it does not literally mean money, *pecunia*, or finances, but, rather, "to trust" or "the act of trusting another." So in fact, Enron/Andersen did fail to fulfill *fiduciary* duties. They broke their bonds of trust with us, and, consequently, we no longer have confidence or trust in them.

Francis Fukuyama, in his important work, *Trust: The Social Virtues and the Creation of Prosperity*, argues that trust is the precondition for prosperity and economic well-being. Fukuyama defines trust as "the expectation that arises within a community of regular, honest, and cooperative behavior, based on shared norms on the part of other members of that community." Robert Solomon and Fernando Flores, in their equally important book *Building Trust*, believe that trust is not only the linchpin for business and commercial arrangements, but that it is the *sine qua non* condition for all interpersonal and social relationships. Like Aristotle, Solomon and Flores argue that trust is the basis of any decent community. At the simple level of survival and stability, people must be able to trust one another in politics, commerce, and battle. Without trust, say Solomon and Flores, neither prosperity nor peaceful polity is possible. Although we are at times cynical, careful, and prudent about what and who we decide to trust, in fact, they argue, life would be impossible or, at the very least, unbearably tedious without a modicum of trust in our day-to-day activities.

> We generally trust the products we buy; we thoughtlessly stake our lives on them (cars, pharmaceuticals, packaged foods, airlines, parachutes, bungee cords). We trust people who serve us, often without checking their credentials. Do most of us ever look at our doctor's or dentist's professional degrees? How do you know that the waitress did not spit in your soup or drop your sandwich on the way from the kitchen? How many people double-check the pills dispensed by their pharmacists? How do we know in an emergency that we haven't hired the Three Stooges as our electricians and plumbers?

What trust boils down to is confidence in the character of another in regard to predictability, reliability, dependability, integrity, and regularity. Trust is a form of freedom. It frees us to seek change; to be open to complexity; to explore new directions, possibilities, and alternatives; and to experiment and express ourselves in our relationships. Although trust always has its limits and always involves risk, trust frees us from the need to continually recheck, rethink, and reanalyze every decision and action that we make.

Fukuyama tells us that without trust, we lose the social capital or social glue necessary for any and all relationships and interactions. In general, Solomon and Flores agree with this metaphor but want to argue that the concept of social capital is a dynamic and not a permanent relationship. They assert that like the words "ethics" and "leadership," "social capital" and "trust" are verbs

Rather, they are part of the
as such, key to business surv
ethics and trust, Solomon a
of leadership is critical. Lea
an "ethical agenda," exempli
"trust in others."

America's Motto

Would you say mo

196

197

198

199

200

* Percen

Think about it: Our econ
mistrust abounds and ethic
damaged. In such a milieu,
play *The Spanish Prisoner*, we
that directly contradicts conf
"Whenever you do business
adversarial relationship and
En Garde!

> Those who really deserve praise are the people who, while human enough to enjoy power nevertheless pay more attention to justice than they are compelled to do by their situation.
>
> **—Thucydides**

Before Richard Grasso's hasty departure from the New York Stock Exchange (after the disclosure of his reportedly $140 million to $185 million pay package), he was fond of exclaiming, "For every Enron, there are 1,000 Exxons." He is, of course, probably right. Even with the subsequent failures at WorldCom, ImClone, Global Crossing, and hundreds of smaller companies that admitted to reporting bogus earnings, Grasso must be right—at least it's statistically probable. But putting numbers aside, isn't part of the issue here one of perception and image as well as names, numbers, and ranking in the Fortune 500? Doesn't the present debacle trigger some very basic questions? Doesn't this present crisis lead us to ask ourselves, Can anyone be trusted? Does anyone have integrity and actually practice what he or she preaches? And what has happened to the notion that leaders should attempt to serve the needs and well-being of the people they lead?

As I said at the beginning of this chapter, Enron and its fellow travelers are only the most recent examples of corporate business failure in regard to ethics, trust, and leadership. There have been others in the past, and, undoubtedly, there will be others in the future. Nevertheless, the magnitude and depth of Enron's perfidy is, to say the least, shocking. John Brennan, chairman and CEO of the Vanguard Group, has suggested that Enron has perhaps forever changed the public's perspective of "business as usual" in the corporate world. Before Enron, he said, people thought that accountants were sacred guardians of financial truth, that CEOs were celebrities and visionaries, and that corporate boards exercised real control over the companies they directed. Sadly, nobody believes much or any of this anymore.

Today's CEOs in the Spotlight	
Dennis Kozlowski, Tyco	Convicted
John Rigas, Adelphia	Convicted
Samuel Waksal, Imclone	Convicted
Bernard Ebbers, Worldcom	Convicted
Richard Scrushy, Health South	Acquitted
Jeffery Skilling, Enron	Indicted
Kenneth Lay, Enron	Indicted
Joe Barardino, Anderson	Resigned

For me, the lesson of Enron is that mistakes, mismanagement, and, yes, malevolence are part of the human condition. There is, I think, no permanent cure for any of this. Sooner or later, everything old is new again. But Enron does serve as a reminder. Leadership, like ethics and trust, exists as a body of knowledge but it truly exists only when practiced face to face. Like medicine, leadership, ethics, and trust are "lived experiences": Learn one, do one, teach one—and so, pass it on.

10. Sex (Yes, Sex)

Lust is but a bloody fire,
Kindled with unchaste desire,
Fed in heart, whose flames aspire
As thoughts do blow them,
Higher and higher!

—**William Shakespeare,** *The Merry Wives of Windsor*

Why do people have sex? *Prima facie*, that question is a no-brainer. It feels good. It's fun. We like it, a lot! And so, we pursue it and do it, as often as possible. Sex is, arguably, humankind's most common and immediate form of pleasure and entertainment. As Mark Twain said, "To the lonely it is company; to the forsaken it is a friend; to the aged and impotent it is a benefactor; they that be penniless are still rich, in that they have this majestic diversion."

Sex can be performed alone, with another person, or in groups. From self-gratification to the basic one-on-one missionary position, to swinging and taking part in orgies—sex is a game that almost any number can play. And, depending on one's personal tastes and preferences, the heights and the depths of sexual pleasure can be achieved in a heterosexual, homosexual, or bisexual manner. Moreover, it is a form of pleasure that doesn't require, but often includes, previous experience, extensive training, gadgets and toys, or drugs and alcohol.

As a species, human beings like sex. We want sex. We even, truth be told, need sex. And, unfortunately, we also are, all too often, seemingly totally driven by sex. There's an old joke that goes something like this: "Question: Why do men always name their *pendentas*? Answer: Because they don't want a complete stranger making all their important life decisions for them!" To be fair, men are not alone in regard to sexual rapaciousness. A recent cover story in *Newsweek*, "The New Infidelity," reported that more women are cheating on their husbands than ever before. Michele Weiner-Davis, a marriage counselor and founder of the Divorce Busting Center in Woodstock, Illinois, said that when she started her practice 20 years ago, just 10 percent of the infidelity cases she knew of involved women's infidelity. Now, she said, it's closer to 50 percent. "Women," says Weiner-Davis, "have suddenly begun to give themselves the same permission to step over the boundary the way men have."

According to sexual critic and author Laura Kipnis, women have discovered the secret that men have known for a long time. Secret sex (sex outside the rules, risky sex) is alive, an adventure, and deliciously dangerous. It is an experiment in physiological positions and technique that is often totally different from one's usual partner. "Adultery," says Kipnis, "is to love-by-the-rules what the test tube is to science: a container for experiments. It's a way to have a hypothesis, to be improvisational. . . . Like any experiment, it might be a really bad idea or it might be a miracle cure. . . . Or it could just fizzle," says Kipnis. "You never really know in advance, do you?" But whether sex is gay or straight, licensed or naughty, monogamous or multitudinous, sex is a very old, very fundamental, very important part of our lives.

> Humans, as mammals, are no different in this regard (sexu-
> ality) from barnyard livestock. Since time immemorial,
> humanity has had no trouble realizing that however much
> some of us might insist on having been created in God's
> image, down deep we are undeniably animals—for we
> hump just like the pigs in the wallow.
>
> **—Niles Eldredge, *Why We Do It***

I remember eagerly signing up for psychology 101 in my first semester in college. The syllabus contained a long list of readings from Sigmund Freud. The titles and topics we would cover included "The Pleasure Principle," "Beyond the Pleasure Principle," "On Intimacy," and "The Libido, the Ego, and the Id." I was really excited (pun intended)! My imagination ran wild! Sex talk! The real stuff. And (I hoped) it would be discussed in graphic detail with lots and lots of pictures and diagrams. No more euphemisms, metaphors, and childish analogies about the birds and the bees. No more parental censorship and Catholic denial and repression. (When I was growing up, the sum total of Catholic teachings on sex could be reduced to one sentence: *Don't do it until you're married, and then only when absolutely necessary!*) But boy, once the class started, was I ever disappointed. There were no pictures, no graphic elements at all, no sordid juicy details, and absolutely no tips about technique or what "cool moves" might actually work on a real live woman. It was all theory and abstract analysis with lots of Greek- and Latin-based terms like the Oedipus complex, narcissism, melancholia, sublimation, and, horror of horrors, erectile dysfunction! There were no bawdy stories or titillating tales whatsoever.

Although I didn't pick up any handy particulars in the class, once I got over my teenage disappointment, I did learn a lot, at least at the level of theory. I found out that Freud directly contradicted the Victorian and medical mores of his times when he asserted the heretical thesis that both our physical and psychological well-being are directly dependent upon the gratification of our conscious and unconscious sexual instincts, desires, and needs.

For Freud, we are driven by the pursuit of pleasure and the fulfillment of our pleasure principle. The pleasure principle is our inborn tendency to seek satisfaction through the discharge of tension and distress, and the primary focus of our satisfaction is sexuality. For Freud, sexuality is not simply physical gratification or "rutting for reproduction." Sexuality encompasses a far greater spectrum than genital gratification. Freud believed that all pleasurable impulses and activities are ultimately sexual in nature, from coitus, to food, to the achievement of power, fame, or social success, to art, music, and even the biological relief and pleasure in the elimination of bodily fluids and waste materials. Freud argued that when our pleasure principle is, for whatever reason, repressed, denied, diminished, or displaced, what results is "libidinal blockage" or the denial of our sexual instinct, which in turn produces any number of negative outcomes, such as anxiety, melancholia, hypochondria, neuroses, personality displacement, regression, and a whole variety of physical, psychological, and sexual perversions.

My professor argued that for Freud, sex and the pursuit of sex, with all of its possible "psychosocial and psychosexual" manifestations, was the mechanism and the pulse of life. He argued that we are ineluctably drawn to it and driven by it. He argued that babies are a by-product of our relentless pursuit of pleasure. For Freud, he said, pleasure is the primary purpose of sex. That is why, he said, only humans and a few other higher hominoids make love for good reason, no reason, or any old reason at all!

In uomini, in soldati sperare fedeltá?

"You expect fidelity in men, in soldiers?"

—Lorenzo de Ponte,
Cosí fan tutte

On reflection, I guess I did learn one practical and personal thing from the class. I learned that it wasn't just I who was so damned preoccupied with sex. It wasn't just I who thought about it constantly. It wasn't just I who yearned for it, prayed for it, plotted out complex campaigns (none of them very successful) to achieve it! Thanks to my professor and Dr. Freud, I now had an excuse for my obsessions. It wasn't just I; it was all part of the human condition. It was great to find out that I was normal. I wasn't a sexual pervert. I was just an average 19-year-old man-child. I was truly relieved. Sexually frustrated, yes, but so relieved!

> In Minnesota, teenage boys think about sex every 17 seconds.
> In big cities, they think about it every 10 seconds. I've
> always been thankful that I grew up in Minnesota. I knew
> I couldn't stand the pressure and pace of city life.
>
> **—Garrison Keillor,** *Prairie Home Companion*

Since graduating from college, I have come to learn that much of Freud's thought, and psychoanalysis itself as a discipline, has undergone intensive scrutiny, criticism, and revision. In hindsight, many scholars now believe that Freud probably over-stated his case a bit. Sex is not likely the single driving force or the exclusive and primary concern of our psyches and personalities. But there's no denying that sex is a part of our "hardwiring," and that the needs, wants, and demands of sex can lead us to ecstasy or debauchery and debasement. As one wag-commentator put it, "To claim that sex does not effect our decision making is to be one of three things: a liar, a castrato, or dead!"

Evolutionary psychology is a relative newcomer to the literature on sex. Evolutionary psychology, like the sociobiology from which it developed, sees the need to spread genes as the organizing principle around which all of animal life and human behavior is constructed. A basic postulate of evolution is that all persistent animal/human behavior has evolved to achieve maximum fitness, adaptation, and survival. Evolutionary success is measured by reproduction, passing on genes, and a sufficient number of offspring to guarantee succeeding generations. The means by which this is achieved is sex. Sex/lust optimizes the possibilities of a good evolutionary outcome. Hence, our interest in sex is a specific solution to the specific problems of survival and reproduction. Therefore, it can be argued that excessive sex, preoccupation with sex, may be redundant, but at the evolutionary level it is a positive or good thing.

Sex may not be the life force or the pulse of life, but it is part of life. Sex is a natural and necessary part of the human psyche. Its drives are strong and real, and the impulse to have sex is not necessarily negative, maladaptive, or wrong. Whatever his errors and excesses, at the very least Freud took sex out of the privacy of the bedroom and brought it out for public scrutiny and debate.

Sex Sells, and People Buy

We live in a sex-saturated society. Between the advertisement industry, movies, magazines, the Internet, television, and other media outlets, we are bombarded with a steady diet of sexual metaphors, messages, allusions, and innuendoes. The simple fact is that sex sells, and we use sex to sell sex itself and all kinds of other products, goods, and services from the plebian to the pornographic.

Fashion Statistics

The percentage of women who point to "hot" celebrities for clothing ideas.*

Age	Percentage
16–24	47%
23–34	26%
35–55	24%
55–70	2%

*Data derived from 3,600 interviews

—*Lifestyle Monitor Magazine* (Cotton Inc.)

In a very real sense, we are, more often than not, literally seduced into consumption. No, it is not necessarily the case that we actually feel sexual satisfaction in purchasing a product or service, although it is possible to do so. But we do often feel "sexy," "cool," "relevant," or "hip" in the purchases we make. In effect, the bottom line here is really the same principle: Sex and sexiness sells!

I think it is fair to argue that the dawn of the complete eroticization of popular culture in America was the turbulent and tumultuous 1960s. Not all of us who came of age in the age of Aquarius smoked dope, went to Woodstock, marched for Civil Rights, saw the original version of *Hair*, and experimented with half of the sexual positions mentioned in the *Kama Sutra*. Some of us did, but most of us didn't. (Sadly, I am in the latter category.) But even if you didn't do all or any of these things, the tenor of the times certainly gave you permission to do so. The explosion in the number of baby boomers going off to college, the feminist movement, the introduction of the Pill, and the mass introduction of recreational drugs created a milieu for experimentation and innovation. Although many baby boomers grew up to be very middle-class in our middle age, lots of us—in our heart of hearts—still feel young, wild, and vital. Even if that vitality now needs to be augmented with Viagra.

In 1953, a nice young man from Chicago and a recent graduate of the University of Illinois started a new business and created a new philosophy of life. His name was Hugh M. Hefner, and both his business and his new philosophy was called Playboy. Hefner launched the first issue of *Playboy* magazine with $600 that he borrowed and approximately $8,000 in stocks in his fledgling company, which he sold to 40 acquaintances. The first issue was put together on Hefner's kitchen table. It featured pictures of an up-and-coming movie starlet named Norma Jean Baker (aka Marilyn Monroe) that Hefner paid $500 to reprint.

Within two weeks of publication, the new magazine had sold out its entire run of 72,000 copies. In 1960, circulation reached one million copies, and at its peak in 1972 it printed more than seven million copies per month. In 2004 *Playboy* had a U.S. total paid circulation of 3.15 million, which is larger than that of *Esquire*, *GQ*, and *Rolling Stone* combined. Almost ten million American adults (82 percent of readers are male, 18 percent female) read *Playboy* each month, and an estimated five million others read the 17 international editions of the magazine. *Playboy* claims to be the most read and best-selling men's magazine in the world. Although *Playboy* broke all the rules and helped to create the guidelines for the creation of a slick, successful sex magazine, by today's standards *Playboy* is stable, staid, and, if not quite a dinosaur, clearly a grandfather in the industry. A quick survey of other men's magazines will reveal a growing list of naughty new magazines bearing outrageous titles (*Maxim, Tease, Moist, Nuts,* and *Screw*) and filled with photos and stories that might make Hefner blush in surprise and embarrassment.

The pervasive medium of our age is, of course, television. In the old days before cable and satellite TV, the transmission of all television images and programming was carefully monitored and controlled by both the Federal Communications Commission (FCC) and the national networks themselves. They established strict guidelines concerning subject matter, language, and levels of violence. According to the Henry J. Kaiser Family Foundation, those days are long gone. In a survey titled "Sex on TV: Content

Top 25 Magazines in Paid Circulation

	Title	Total
1.	*Modern Maturity*	17,183,768
2.	*Reader's Digest*	11,944,898
3.	*TV Guide*	9, 061,639
4.	*Better Homes and Gardens*	7,607,832
5.	*National Geographic*	6,657,424
6.	*Good Housekeeping*	4,690,508
7.	*Family Circle*	4,601,708
8.	*Women's Day*	4,246,805
9.	*Time*	4,109,962
10.	*Ladies' Home Journal*	4,101,414
11.	*People Weekly*	3,632,804
12.	*Rosie*	3,337,582
13.	*Sports Illustrated*	3,245,940
14.	*Playboy*	3,213,638
15.	*Prevention*	3,150,017
16.	*Newsweek*	3,125,151
17.	*Cosmopolitan*	3,021,720
18.	*Guideposts*	2,656,622
19.	*Southern Living*	2,562,757
20.	*Maxim*	2,512,090
21.	*Seventeen*	2,459,135
22.	*Redbook*	2,394,184
23.	*Martha Stewart Living*	2,359,328
24.	*Glamour*	2,304,151
25.	*O, the Oprah Magazine*	2,261,570

—*Adweek*, **March 10, 2003**

and Context," the Kaiser Foundation reported that nearly two-thirds of general-audience TV programming includes sexual content and that more than four in five shows contain sexual messages, themes, and topics. Though the survey concluded that most TV sex was moderate—passionate kissing and touching—one in every seven programs contains sexual intercourse, whether by depicting it directly or by portraying characters who are about to begin or have just finished having sex. (One positive finding of the survey is that 25 percent of the shows that depicted or discussed intercourse also included references to safe sex.)

Nature of Sexual Content on TV, By Genre

	Any Sexual Content	Avg. Scenes per hr.	Any Talk about Sex	Avg. Scenes per hr.	Any Sexual Behavior	Avg. Scenes per hr.
Soap Opera	96%	5.1	92%	4.0	70%	2.6
Movie	87%	3.7	80%	2.8	74%	1.9
Comedy Series	73%	7.8	71%	7.4	32%	3.6
Drama Series	71%	4.6	69%	4.1	35%	2.1
Talk Show	65%	4.0	65%	4.0	0%	0.0
News Magazine	53%	2.3	53%	2.3	7%	*
Reality	28%	4.5	27%	4.4	5%	2.2
Total	64%	4.4	27%	3.8	32%	2.1

* Too few to provide a good estimate

Source: Henry J. Kaiser Family Foundation

With the advent of cable and satellite TV, of course, everything changed. Cable and satellite TV did not use the public electronic spectrum and therefore were not under the purview of the FCC. Cable and satellite TV are subscription services, and so two basic axioms of capitalism apply: (1) "If it is not specifically forbidden, it is allowed! (Hence nudity, vulgarity, and violence are fair game.) (2) *Caveat emptor*, "Let the buyer beware!" (Hence HBO's motto, warning, and promise: "This is not TV, this is HBO!")

Even the Ads on TV Have Changed

Erectile dysfunction is no longer a forbidden topic of discussion. Erectile dysfunction advertising has grown substantially in recent years. In January of 2004 during the Super Bowl, *Levitra*, *Viagra*, and *Cialis* all ran ads proclaiming the physical and psychological benefits of using their products. In 2003, *Viagra* and *Levitra* spent $118 million on advertising. In 2004 marketing executives at *Cialis* plan to spend in excess of $100 million to help *expand* their sales.

—Crain Communications, Inc., April 5, 2004

Cable and satellite TV have forever changed what comes into our homes, and perhaps what now constitutes family viewing. Subscription TV can run uncensored and uncut movies and films without concern for their X or R ratings. And of course they can produce their own shows, some of which would make Sam Peckinpah (*The Wild Bunch* [graphic stylized violence]),

Russ Meyers (*Vixon* and *Beyond the Valley of the Dolls* [soft-core porn]), and George Carlin (*Seven Dirty Words*: s___, p___, f___, c___, c_____r, m_____r, and t____), proud, happy, and green with envy. The two classic examples of this phenomenon are, of course, HBO's blockbuster hits *Sex and the City* and *The Sopranos*. And let's not forget that cable and satellite TV also have the ability to directly distribute adult pornographic programming to viewers who pay an additional fee above basic monthly rates. In 2003, for example, Comcast, the nation's largest cable company, pulled in more than $50 million from adult programming.

> Unfortunately, even in an age of AIDS, sex is commercially marketed as adult play, primarily pleasurable, and with little or no reference to safe or responsible sexual conduct. And yet, according to an article in the *Herald International Tribune* (July 10/11, 2004), the death toll from AIDS continues to be staggeringly high:
>
> "In the past 20 years, approximately 60 million people have been infected with HIV; 20 million have died. Eight thousand people—nearly three times 9/11's death toll—die of AIDS every day. By 2010, experts predict 100 million infections worldwide and 25 million AIDS orphans."

According to CBS's *60 Minutes*, pornography is one of the oldest businesses in the world, and now, thanks to videos, DVDs, and the Internet, business has never been better. It is estimated that Americans now spend around $10 billion a year on adult entertainment, which is as much as they spend attending professional sporting events, buying music, or going to the movies. According to the *60 Minutes* report, in 2002 alone, the pornographic film industry churned out 11,000 new titles, and there were more than 800 million rentals of pornographic videotapes and DVDs in video stores across the nation.

And then there's the Internet. Too embarrassed to walk into a store to rent *Debbie Does Dallas, Deep Throat,* or *Behind the Green Door?* No problem. Now, thanks to the Internet, there are potentially 70 million to 80 million households in the United States that have their own "totally private" adult porn entertainment centers. Moreover, there are in excess of 1.3 million porn websites and chat rooms, which contain 260 million web pages of pornographic material. According to a published report by Reuters (June 4, 2004), online porn sites get three times more visits than all the top search engines, including market leader, Google. A child's advocacy group, Protecting Children in Cyberspace, claims that sex is the number one searched-for topic on the Internet, and that the cybersex industry generates $1 billion annually and is expected to grow $5 to $7 billion a year over the next five years. The bottom line in all of this is obvious. For good or ill, sexual standards have changed, and they keep changing. As a recent article in the *New York Times* pointed out, to a generation raised on Britney Spears, Internet porn, Monica Lewinsky, and *Sex and the City,* oral sex isn't real sex, it's just oral!

Our Hypersexual Puritan Heritage

A surprising human and cultural irony that is highlighted by our media-based age is that although we live in a sex-saturated society, we are not necessarily comfortable with sexuality. Historically, we have been steadfastly of two minds about the topic of sexuality in all of its both pleasurable and pedestrian manifestations. We find sex both titillating and problematic. At one and the same time, says Laura Kipnis, we live in a culture that is "hypersexual" and yet puritanical in its beliefs and mythologies regarding sex and the body.

> Sex! The pleasure is momentary, the positions ridiculous, and the expense damnable.
>
> **—Lord Chesterfield, English statesman and writer**

In Western Christian thought, the body has always been an obstacle to human growth and salvation. The body was seen as the "lesser thing," this "corporeal prison" that impedes and confuses the life of the mind and the perfection of the soul. St. Francis of Assisi referred to his body as "his brother ass," the encasement that housed his spirit and soul. From the story of Adam and Eve and their expulsion from paradise, the body has been perceived as part of humankind's painful penalty for disobeying the word of God. The body is but flesh. It produces wastes. It is unclean. The body is demanding. It must be fed. It must be maintained. The body is but mortal. It is susceptible to corruption, disease, and death.

Western philosophy, from the time of the Greeks, was also uncomfortable with our "corporeal nature" and preferred the *psyche* (mind) over the *sōma* (body). For Aristotle, Plato, and Socrates, the acts of reasoning and contemplation were the highest activities of the human condition. The pleasures of the body, sensuality, and eros distracted us, drained us of energy, and, hence, were to be seen as enemies of reason. They believed that reason could free us from the imprisonment of the body and the limits of our emotions, feelings, and desires.

The demonization of the body perhaps found its most ardent support in the works of Augustine of Hippo and Thomas Aquinas. For Augustine, the good soul finds itself imprisoned, trapped in the bad body, and that the pleasures of the body were the chief source of all our problems. We must, he argued, triumph over our animal natures and free ourselves from sexual desire. The only possible excuse for sex, said Augustine, is procreation, which should be indulged in without lust or pleasure. Aquinas, like Augustine, argued that sex is permitted only for procreation. Aquinas routinely associated intercourse with such terms as—filth, stain, foulness, vileness, and distaste. He believed that any sexual activity or desire that does not have reproduction as its aim is unclean, ungodly, and immoral.

The essential point I'm trying to make in this chapter is that, quiet ironically, sex is yet another way to avoid ethical considerations and reinforce the "fortress of self." Although we may experience some hesitancy and schizophrenia in its regard, the almost total eroticization of our commercial culture makes sexuality, in all of its possible forms, a convenient, easy, and immediate method of remaining ensconced in the *emotional maze of our own narcissism.* Sex allows us to lose ourselves in the moment. It allows us to forget, to cope, to overcome, to endure. It allows us a diversion. It allows us to escape. It anesthetizes us. It buffers us from other considerations and concerns. When sex is used in this manner it becomes, at best, a private challenge, a game, an athletic event, a biological function, a release, an endorphin high. It is a self-centered act, which is insensitive to the desires and pleasures of any possible partner. Sex of this kind denies the subjectivity and autonomy of another, using the person as a mere instrument for one's own gratification. Sex of this kind alienates us from ourselves and others. Sex of this kind desires desire and/or seeks to simply sate an appetite. Sex of this kind may not necessarily be about the domination and conquest of another, but it is about selfishness, using others, and escapism.

The Seven Deadly Sins

Sloth, Greed, Gluttony, Anger, Envy, Pride, Lust

The Seven Heavenly Virtues

Prudence, Temperance, Justice, Fortitude, Faith, Hope, Charity

---

The Dignity of Lust

Simon Blackburn writes in his elegant and interesting recent book, *Lust*, that sex need not and should not solely be about self.

Blackburn argues that traditionally we have lumped sex and lust together and have given them both a bad name which they do not deserve. For Blackburn, lust need not be excessive, illicit, or dehumanizing. Lust can be a virtue and not a vice. Lust, when properly understood and performed, is, in the words of David Hume, "useful or agreeable to the person himself and to others."

Lust is about desire that is felt. It is palpable. It floods the body, the mind, the heart. Lust is not cerebral or simply imagined. Lust is desire that arouses the senses and the body. Lust is, says Blackburn, enthusiastic desire for sexual activity for its own sake. Lust is not *necessarily* about the expression of eternal romantic love. Lust is not *always* an attempt to impregnate. Lust is about the pursuit of sexual ecstasy for itself alone. *But, but, but*, says Blackburn, the full pleasure of sexual activity requires the presence of another, a partner, a fellow traveler. There must always be an object of lust: a "partner," an "other" who is not treated as other, but rather as someone you "desire to please" as much as you "desire to be pleased."

Citing Thomas Hobbes, Blackburn argues that lust is about two drives or two appetites together: *To please < — > To be pleased*. "I desire you, and I desire your desire for me. . . . A pleases B, B is pleased at what A is doing and A is pleased at B's pleasure." And, so on, and so on, and so on. As Hobbes put this point, "The appetite which men call Lust . . . is sensual pleasure, but not only that; there is in it also a delight of the mind: for it consisteth of two appetites together, to please, and to be pleased; and the delight men take in delighting, is not sensual, but a pleasure or joy of mind, consisting in the imagination of the power they have so much to please."

For Blackburn, true lust must be more than one-sided. Lust is about communion, harmony, completion. "The subject is not centrally pleased at himself," says Blackburn, "but at the excitement of the other. . . . There are no cross-purposes, hidden agendas, mistakes, or deceptions. Lust here is like making music together, a joint symphony of pleasure and response. There is a pure mutuality."

Blackburn believes that we should not be "enemies of lust." "Lust," he contends, is not merely useful, but essential. "We would none of us be here without it." Moreover, he suggests that lust, if properly pursued and applied, is an ethical act because it requires us to step outside the fortress of self and take into consideration the feelings, needs, and desires of others. (In a post-AIDS world, this would include issues of safe sex as well as satisfying sex with one's partner.) It behooves us, says Blackburn, "to speak up for lust," "to restore lust to humanity," to lift lust "from the category of a sin to that of a virtue."

The most difficult task of romantic life: Getting *Like, Love,* and *Lust* all in one relationship

11. Death (Ditto)

It is natural to ask why—Why am I here rather than there?
Why am I now rather than then? Why am I at all?

—**Pascal**

Ah, mon cher, for anyone who is alone, without God and
without a master, the weight of days is dreadful. Hence
one must choose a master, God being out of style.

—**Albert Camus**

In Homer's *Iliad,* the warrior-hero Achilles, in a moment of
self-reflection on his life as a man of action, muses that the gods
envy humankind because we are mortal and everything we do is
acutely "now." For Achilles, the game of life is engaging because
the possibility of death makes our every action vital, interesting,
and intense. Achilles' bravura is, of course, only a sham and a
show of daring. The gods may, in fact, experience momentary
jealousy about the immediacy of our lives, but their final revenge
on us makes their displeasure easily endurable. For the gods
know the true irony behind Achilles' braggadocio. Men do deeds
of daring out of desperation as much as desire, because we seek to

overcome, if only for a moment, our fear of the finality of death and the obscurity of the grave. As Samuel Johnson said, "The prospect of death wonderfully concentrates the mind."

Ernest Becker, in his 1973 classic, *The Denial of Death*, argues that the "primary mainspring" of human action is not the pursuit of sex, as Freud proposed, but, rather, the pursuit of "distractions" that will counterbalance our overwhelming fear of the immensity of eternity and the awareness of our finitude. As a species, human beings have a basic existential dilemma: We are both burdened and blessed with a paradoxical nature, half animal and half symbolic. That means, for Becker, that we are simultaneously aware of the *possibility* of infinity and the absolute *certainty* that we are finite. We live our whole lifetimes, said Becker, with the "fate of death haunting our dreams" on even the "most sun-filled days."

> This is the paradox: [man] is out of nature and hopelessly in it; he is dual, up in the stars and yet housed in a heart-pumping, breath-gasping body that once belonged to a fish and still carries the gill-marks to prove it. His body is a material fleshy casing that is alien to him in many ways—the strangest and most repugnant way being that it aches and bleeds and will decay and die. Man is literally split in two: he has an awareness of his own splendid uniqueness in that he sticks out of nature with a towering majesty, and yet he goes back into the ground a few feet in order to blindly and dumbly rot and disappear forever.

The idea of death, says Becker, the fear of it, haunts us like nothing else. It is the "motivating principle" (mainspring) of human activity. And all human activity is consciously and unconsciously designed to deny and combat our fear and terror of death. According to William James, death is "the worm at the core" of our pretensions to happiness. No matter how much we try to lose ourselves in the moment, no matter how much we distract ourselves and keep ourselves busy, "the evil background [of death] is really there to be thought of," James says, "and the skull will grin in at the banquet."

The "painful riddle of death" haunts us, says Becker, causing us mental and physical grief and despair. Our fear wears us out, and so, says Becker, we seek, out of necessity, to repress it, sublimate it, take it off the table of our immediate sense of consciousness. We create mental defenses, illusions, myths, stories, tasks, crusades, causes, work, rituals, and bizarre behaviors to distract us from our discomfort and despair. "Reality is the misery," says Becker, so if we cannot defeat it and deny it, we at least can create actions and ideas that offer us a defense against despair, our dread of death, and the overwhelming realities of life. Full humanness, says Becker, without the filters and distractions, means fear, trembling, and certain madness: "This is the terror: to have emerged from nothing, to have a name, consciousness of self, deep inner feelings, an excruciating inner yearning for life and self-expression—and with all this yet to die."

Although we all desire to overcome our "basic creatureliness," says Becker, we know we cannot. We are born to die. We are in fact condemned to die by God's own words to Adam in the Garden of Eden. "Because you (Adam) ate of the fruit of the tree of knowledge—thou shalt surely die." Rather than trying to overcome our basic creatureliness, says Becker, we seek to "repress our fear of our fate." If this fear of our ultimate fate were constantly conscious to us, said Becker, we would be unable to function normally. To have a modicum of comfort, to have a chance of enjoying our lives, we need not master death per se, but we must master our fear of death. We must act in a way that suggests to ourselves and others that we are able to live without thinking about our own deaths. We must repress our fear and live as if we were immortal, as if death were only an intellectual possibility and not a biological certainty.

> If a man were a beast or an angel, he would not be able to
> be in dread [because he would be unselfconscious]. Since
> he is a synthesis he can be in dread. . . . [M]an himself pro-
> duces dread.
>
> **—Søren Kierkegaard**

Perhaps the most traditional way to avoid, deny, and/or repress the thoughts of death ("unto dust thou shalt return") is through religion. According to Karen Armstrong, there is a case to be made that we are not only rational beings (*Homo sapiens*) but also spiritual beings (*Homo religiosus*). Men and women, says Armstrong, started to worship gods as soon as they became recognizably human. They did this, she says, not just because they wanted to "propitiate powerful forces." Rather, she says, these early faiths were an attempt to find meaning, value, and direction in this beautiful but nonetheless painful, terrifying, and mysterious world. Successful religions, says Armstrong, are, for all their otherworldliness, highly pragmatic in function. They need not be logically or scientifically sound, but they must help us make life more bearable. They must offer us a meaning, or a purpose, or an explanation for our lives, or, at the very least, they must offer us a form of "aesthetic anesthesia" that comforts us and allows us to endure. The bottom line for Armstrong is that religion must offer a "consoling creed."

Becker agrees that, generally speaking, religion is an attempt to offer answers to the *mysterium tremendum* of life. All religions, says Becker, offer explanations, meaning, symbolism, rituals, and organizational principles. But at the core of all major historical religions, says Becker, is an attempt to address the problem of how to deal with death. Most, but not all, major religions offer its followers "an immunity bath" from death: "life after death," "eternal life," "paradise," "valhalla," "heaven."

What religions and a belief in God promise us, says Becker, is a defense against despair, links to "ultimate power," and the possibility of infinitude. The credos of most religions offer us comfort. They communicate to us that our very creatureliness has some meaning to the Creator. They tell us that despite our true insignificance, our existence has meaning "in some ultimate sense because it exists within an eternal and infinite scheme of things brought about and maintained to some kind of design by some creative force."

> I think people believe in heaven because they don't like the idea of dying, because they want to carry on living and they don't like the idea that other people will move into their house and put their things into the rubbish.
>
> —**Mark Haddon**, *The Curious Incident of the Dog in the Night-Time*

The promise of religion, says Becker, is that we are not just "food for worms." Yes, our flesh will die. Yes, we will, because our spirits are encased in our bodies, experience some fear and anxiety. But the sacred commitment of religion is that "we will die to be born again." We will die to this life in order to ascend to another. In some sense, says Becker, for the "true believer," death is the "ultimate promotion," the final elevation to a higher form of life, to the enjoyment of eternity in some form."

Given Becker's thesis regarding our fear of death and our desperate need to deny it, religion can be construed as a benign and relatively harmless answer to the mystery of life. Or it may be so, that is, if our faith option and theological point of view are not zealously myopic, misogynistic, or xenophobic in their interactions with others. The obvious danger in any body of belief or rigidly or strictly defined organizational group is that they can become incredibly isolated from others, seeing all outsiders as "different," "not like us," and/or "potential adversaries." When and if this happens, a kind of collective narcissism can occur. From an individual point of view it is difficult enough to overcome the "imperatives of self," but from a collective point of view it may be impossible to step away from the peer pressure, group-think, and collective survival anxiety of one's fellow believers and congregants. What can occur is an us-against-them mentality: Catholics v. Protestants, Jews v. Muslims, Missouri Synod Lutherans v. Evangelical Lutherans, Hindus v. Sikhs, Shiahs v. Sufis, Hasidics v. Reforms, Unitarians v. Ethical Humanists, Red Sox fans v. Yankee fans (kidding!).

> Groups have never thirsted after truth. They demand illusions, and cannot do without them. They constantly give what is unreal precedence over what is real; they are almost as strongly influenced by what is untrue as by what is true.
>
> **—Sigmund Freud**

A less lofty way to elude thoughts of mortality, says Becker, is to mindlessly lose ourselves in the minutia of the mundane. Lifting a page from Søren Kierkegaard, Becker laments that most of us use the "normal neurosis of philistinism," that is, "we tranquilize ourselves with the trivial" in order to avoid dwelling on the inevitable. For Kierkegaard, philistinism is a method of dealing with life that allows us to be lulled and contented by the daily routines and ordinary satisfactions that society offers: "Devoid of imagination, as the Philistine always is, he lives in a certain trivial province of experience as to how things go, what is possible, what usually occurs. . . . Philistinism tranquilizes itself in the trivial." Becker argues that in today's world, the car, the shopping center, our jobs, our things, and the two-week summer vacation preoccupy our thoughts and motivate our actions. We are, says Becker, protected and insulated against reality by the secure and limited alternatives that society offers us. And, "if we do not look up from this path," we can live out our lives with a certain blessed ignorance and "dull security."

Becker writes that the most dramatic way to deny the terror of death is to act as if fear means nothing to us and that we are not helpless and abandoned in the world and fated for oblivion. If life is "dumb to us," if there is no menu or logical set of directions from which we may seek advice and select options, if we are, seemingly, on our own and left to our own devices, then our only alternative is to thrash out, to act. If we cannot beat death, we can at least temporarily ignore and deny it through culturally sanctioned heroic acts as well as outrageous acts of violence and evil. For Becker, it is only in choosing to act that we assert our "being" and, at least temporarily, overcome "nothingness." Heroism, he writes, "is first and foremost a reflex of terror and death. We admire most the courage to face death; we give such valor our highest and most constant adoration; it moves us deeply in our hearts because we have doubts about how brave we ourselves would be. . . . Man has elevated animal courage to a cult."

Becker argues that the "hero project" is a pose, a learned character trait, a grand illusion, and a "neurotic defense against despair." In the "hero project," we put on the "character armor" (Wilhelm Reich's term) of the action hero, "lay away" our fears, and pretend to make the world more manageable. Like William James' notion of "acting oneself into being," the hero, through his or her actions, seeks reinforcement of self, recognition, unabashed self-esteem, ersatz immortality, and, if possible, cosmic significance.

I believe that Becker offers at least three models of heroes. First is the classic hero who risks and/or sacrifices him or herself for a greater communal cause—the group, the state, or the nation—or in the pursuit of a collective sense of honor, justice, or truth. This category of heroes covers a wide range of possibilities: the athlete, the martyr, the leader, the sage, the saint, the scientist, and, of course, the warrior.

The second category is the conventional hero. This category of hero also "aches for cosmic specialness" but seeks it in a more mundane manner. Instead of killing on the field of battle, these heroes strive to make a killing in business. Instead of being nationally known personalities, they disguise their need to transcend the ordinary and deny death by staying busy and staying focused. They fixate on making money, getting a better home in a nicer neighborhood, buying a big car, sending their kids to more prestigious colleges and universities. They measure their sense of heroism by financial success and peer-group recognition.

The third hero paradigm is what Becker calls "the meaner side of man's urge to cosmic heroism": "ignoble heroics" or "antiheroism." Just as heroic actions allow us public acclaim, self-esteem, and a temporary respite from our fear of death, so too, says Becker, do actions that are negative, cruel, and evil in their intent. These actions, says Becker, are also techniques for earning recognition and glory. The bully, the thug, the crook, and the corrupt politician may not be loved or admired, but they are recognized, and, like it or not, they have to be reckoned with. The ignoble behavior of such antiheroes as Charles Manson, Reverend Jim Jones, Stalin, and Hitler guaranteed their place in history, if only in the pantheon of the despicable and damned. A slightly more bearable and acceptable example of the antihero in popular culture today is a TV character by the name of Tony Soprano.

Finding Meaning in Being Bad

As I mentioned in chapter 6, we have long loved the rough-neck, the rascal, and the bad boy in both our films and our literature. We seem to be drawn to their flair for the dangerous, their willingness to take a risk, their outrageousness and daring. Of course, our infatuation with these "bad boys" and "pirate kings" has its limits. We do not want, nor are we easily drawn, in fiction or in fact, to antiheroes who were sadists, serial killers, or ghouls. The Marquis de Sade, Jeffrey Dahmer, and John Wayne Gacy may evoke our curiosity, but their conduct and behavior is too ghastly for them to qualify as lovable rascals or even rascals whom we love to hate. (Nevertheless, Becker claims that the actions of a de Sade, Dahmer, and Gacy—for all their horror—are still nothing more than *their twisted attempts* to cope with their own sense of mortality.) For us to relate to antiheroes, they need to be both scary and lovable, and they need to find a balance between being naughty and nice, tough and soft, strong and compassionate. The creator of *The Sopranos*, David Chase, has intentionally fashioned just such an antihero in his main character, Anthony "Tony" Soprano.

In his mid-forties, Tony Soprano is a second-generation wise guy. Although he tells his neighbors, his children's teachers, and the IRS that he is in waste management, in fact he is the acting boss of the most powerful criminal organization in New Jersey. Tony likes his work and loves his life, both professionally and personally—at least, when he can keep them all properly separated, balanced, and under control. Tony is a big, powerful, physical man with even bigger appetites for good wine, good food, good cigars, and sex—whether with his Russian *goomah* (girlfriend), a quickie at the strip club the *Bada Bing*, or, on occasion, even with his wife. In his interactions with his family, friends, and associates, he is by turn benign or brutal, selfish or sensitive, lecherous or loving, overwhelmingly physical or psychologically insightful. Like the heroine in Erica Jong's *Fear of Flying*, Tony's general outlook on life is that of an alpha warrior/hunter: "The world is a predatory place, take big bites, eat faster!"

A major piece of the dramatic tension of *The Sopranos* comes out of just how much Tony likes the life of being a "wise guy," a "made man," a *capo di capo*. The other guys—Paulie Walnuts, Big Pussey, Christopher, Silvio, and Furio—aren't just his employees or even his fellow workers. They are his crew, his tribe, his truest family. These are the guys he plays with, fights and argues with, steals with, makes war and kills with, and, if need be, would die with. These are the men with whom he shares his real life—life on the street, life on the hustle. Tony likes his gang, and he likes the games they play to get by: gambling, racketeering, union scams, stolen property, loan sharking. He likes the dreaming, the scheming, the game playing, the con, the heist. He likes the risks and the dangers. He likes the chances they take to put food on the table and, most important in their eyes, prove their manhood. Being a tough guy makes him somebody. Being a tough guy keeps him busy, keeps him preoccupied, keeps him from thinking about death.

As a second-generation mob guy, Tony chose "the life" because he wanted it. Although he regularly preaches the line that Italians were forced into "the life" because they had no other

choice, neither he nor his daughter, Meadow, is entirely convinced. "Right, Dad! Italians had no other choice. Just like Mario
Cuomo, huh, Dad?" Nevertheless, Tony wants to rationalize
his choices and actions by saying he is a man of honor, doing
his job. As far as he's concerned, he's fulfilling his duty. In his
mind, he's just a businessman trying to get by and do well for his
family. But protestations aside, Tony's claims in regard to honor,
duty, and family simply do not pass the litmus test for the code
of honor described by Mario Puzo in regard to Tony's cinematic
predecessor, Don Vito Corleone.

According to Puzo, Vito Corleone was an accidental if not
a reluctant Don. He was not a man who sought the title, and
he embraced it only when circumstances and necessity forced it
upon him. As a child, Vito came to this country as an orphan on
the run from a blood feud in Sicily. As he grew into adulthood,
his hopes and aspirations were modest: a wife, a family, and an
honest job. It was only when a local member of the Black Hand
forced him out of his job and began to harass his friends that the
young Corleone took action. He killed this "Black Hand," this
"fellow Italian who stole from other Italians," out of a sense of
duty and justice and not for personal gain or in an attempt to
establish a reputation. Vito Corleone became a "man of honor"
(*un uomo d'onore*) because he acted on principle and not out of
impulse. Even at the end of his life, sitting in his garden talking to
his son Michael, Vito Corleone felt he had done what was necessary to do. "I make no apologies for my life. What I did, I had

to do. I did it for my family." No such motives can be associated with Tony Soprano's career choice. His selection of a vocation came from the adrenaline rush he got out of watching the strong-arm and bully tactics of his father "Johnny Boy" and his uncle "Junior" Soprano. Honor and ethnic pride aside, Tony sought out, chose, and eagerly embraced "the life" because it looked like fun. For him, it was all about the thrill of the game: the hunt, the chase, the catch.

Perhaps the central issue and overriding existential tension of the entire *Sopranos* series is best captured in the lamentation of Tony's nephew, Christopher Moltisanti: "The f____' regularness of life is too f____' hard on me." Christopher, at the time, is just a soldier and not yet a "made guy," and he desperately wants to be somebody. He wants recognition. He wants to be a player. He wants to overcome the "nothingness" of being an average guy, a working stiff, a nobody. He wants what Tony wants, what all the guys in the gang want: recognition, *stugots* (balls). Christopher wants to be *igualio* (a man among men), one of the boys, one of the crew, a member of the tribe.

Psychiatrist Glen O. Gabbard perfectly captures the collective psyche of Tony's mob by referring to them as a "band of lost boys" who suffer from a sense of existential meaningless-ness and fear being doomed to an unheralded and unobserved life—a mediocre middle-class existence, life as a pawn and not a player. So they individually and collectively seek meaning and self through boisterous activity, violence, and criminal behavior, including murder. In breaking the rules and in their almost total disregard for the rights of others, says Gabbard, they achieve status, possessions, and success, and thereby overcome the numbing sense of absurdity, boredom, and ennui that pervades their lives.

Becker contends that all humanly caused evil and/or heroic acts are nothing more than attempts to deny our creatureliness (mortality) and overcome our insignificance (meaninglessness). Hence to act, to be bold, to achieve hero or antihero status is to achieve at least a modicum of immortality. In so doing, we overcome our humdrum lives and, at least for a while, put away our fears of dying and being forgotten. Like the "lost boys" of William Golding's *Lord of the Flies*, Tony's "band of boys" with more *stugots* than savvy pursue a lifestyle that, while destructive and dysfunctional, distracts them from the dread of dwelling on their own personal sense of insignificance and eventual demise.

Staying Young while Growing Old

I have always known that no one can live forever,
but I had hoped in my case that an exception would be made.

—William Saroyan

There is at least one corollary to Becker's argument regarding the denial of death that is worth consideration. I am referring to our fear of getting old, the cult of youth, our pursuit of agelessness, our desperate attempts to prove wrong what Francis Bacon said: "Age will not be defied."

Myths about Aging

1. People over 65 are old.

2. Most older people are chronically poor in health.

3. Older minds are not as bright and flexible as younger minds.

4. Older people are undependable and unproductive.

5. Older people are unattractive and sexless.

6. All older people are pretty much the same.

7. All older people lose their passion for life.

—Ken Dychtwald, gerontologist

The 2000 census statistics depict a demographic reality I doubt even futurists such as Jules Verne or George Orwell could have foreseen. Not only are more of us living than ever before (281.4 million), more of us are living longer than ever before. In 1900, the average life expectancy in America was 47 years old, and in 2000, the average was 76. And we are not only living longer, we are growing older as a nation. Fully 50.4 percent of our population, or 142.1 million people, are now 35 years old or older. The average age of an American is now 35.3 years old, which is 2.4 years older than the average age a decade ago and 12 years older than a century ago.

Not only have the raw numbers changed, but how we perceive age and how we react to it have been dramatically altered because we are living not only longer but also healthier, more

Seasons of a Man's Life
Daniel Levinson
1978

Late Adulthood	65 —|—	
		Late Adulthood (60—)
Late Adult Transition	60 —|—	
End of Middle Adulthood	55 —|—	
Age 50 Transition	50 —|—	
Middle Adult Entering		Middle Adulthood (40–60)
	45 —|—	
Mid-Life Transition	40 —|—	
Settling Down (Doing, Achieving)	33 —|—	
Early Adult World		Early Adult (17–40)
	22 —|—	
Early Adult Transition	17 —|—	
Childhood & Adolescence		Pre-Adulthood (0–17)

active lives than ever before. In the 1930s, H. L. Mencken lamented that after you're 40 years old, it's all over. "The best years are the 40's," he said. "After that, a person begins to deteriorate. But in their 40's, people are at the zenith of their energy and vitality." For Mencken, 40 meant middle age, and middle age meant crisis, breakdown, and the beginning of old age and death. Not so anymore!

In 1978, the psychologist Daniel J. Levinson in his landmark book *Seasons of a Man's Life* created a chronology, a timeline, a yardstick by which we measure and delineate the different phases in human development. (Although Levinson's thesis primarily dealt with males, many of his theories, life patterns, and developmental models also apply to women.) Levinson postulated that human life was divided into four distinct life stages: Pre-Adulthood (0–17), Early Adulthood (17–40), Middle Adulthood (40–60), and Late Adulthood (60–?).

Though considered cutting-edge at the time of its publication, Levinson's chronology of human development and decline seems in retrospect to be not only a tad gender-biased but also archaic and pessimistic in regard to the numbers. Specifically, Levinson's Late Adulthood is made up of two stages. Stage I, Late Adulthood: Transition (60–65), was about *settling in* and *settling up* accounts. It was about finding satisfaction or disappointment in our lifestyles and life choices. It was about carrying on and doing one's duty or falling apart. Stage II, Late Adulthood (65–?), was, said Levinson, final accounting time. It was about memories, reflections, preparing for death. For Levinson, anything and everything that happened after 65 was seen as a bonus or a perk. Soon after 65, only death awaits.

Personally, I don't think Levinson's numbers or chronology were either myopic or intentionally maudlin. They were simply a reflection of his data and his experience. Nevertheless, whether intentional or not, his research did help to perpetuate the myth that elderly people were frail, useless, unproductive, and finished. In so doing, he reinforced our traditional and unrealistic fear about aging.

Within 20 years of the publication of *Seasons of a Man's Life*, demographic surveys and research began to report on a new

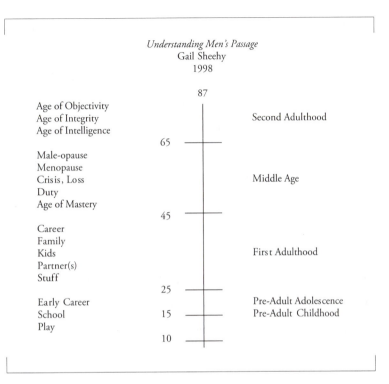

Understanding Men's Passage
Gail Sheehy
1998

timeline for human development and offer a new perspective on aging. In 1998, Gail Sheehy published *Understanding Men's Passages: Discovering the New Map of Men's Lives*, and in 1999, the MacArthur Foundation Research Network released a report on *Successful Midlife Development*. Both of these publications paint a new portrait of aging and offer new models, metaphors, and maps to help plan and navigate our newly extended lives.

Sheehy's timeline not only updates Levinson's numbers but also redefines our lifestyle choices and options as we age. She argues that thanks to advances in general medicine, nutrition, biotechnology, and brain research, we will be routinely able to feeling good about ourselves: "Free your inner child," "Pull your own psychic-levers," "Love yourself," "Eat right," "Get into your body," "Study your dreams," "Become a vessel of acceptance." And, let me add, if a trip to the bookstore doesn't depress you, stop by your local drugstore, where you can now find and purchase any of about 40 kinds of antidepressants to relieve your anxiety, raise your spirits, and keep you centered in your search for happiness and the good life. (European colleagues now tell me that thanks to the Internet, the movie industry, and market globalization, the U.S. fetish regarding the "pursuit of happiness" is now our single largest export.)

Even though there is no exact science to happiness, no set of absolute principles to study, its illusory nature does not deter us. We believe that happiness, whatever it is, is the *summum bonum* ("the ultimate good") of life. Psychologist David G. Myers, who has studied happiness (aka "life satisfaction") for more than 30 years, points out a number of paradoxes regarding its pursuit and achievement. Too many of us, says Myers, believe that happiness is primarily about *things* and *self-centered* behavior. The prevalent attitude is "If I only had (more money, a new car, a bigger house, more clothes, a more prestigious job), I'd be happy!" Or, "I can't be happy because of (poverty, ill health, bad luck, poor schooling)!" Myers argues that the pursuit and the achievement of happiness is not a singular, solitary, and self-centered activity. Happiness, says Myers, always occurs in the context of others and very often with the cooperation of others.

Happiness, different from capitalism, is not a zero-sum game (that is, one that says that if I achieve happiness, you cannot be happy). Happiness, like laughter, is primarily a collective, communal event. Nevertheless, says Myers, too many of us pursue happiness as if we were in competition with others, as if it were in limited supply. And because of this, we focus on self, disregarding others, and play the game only to win regardless of the consequences. Folk wisdom tells us, says Myers, that in the competition for happiness, what matters is success, not ethical sensitivity.

John Dewey was right: We have made a fetish out of the cult of "rugged individualism" and the "pursuit of happiness." We think that all of our rights are personal, private, and proprietary when in fact private rights always and only exist within the context of the collective community. Each generation needs to learn to forget itself on purpose, to let go of its ego needs, to step back from center stage, and at the very least to be open to the voices and the needs of others. Simple prudence (to govern and discipline ourselves by the care of reason) should make us aware that we are not the only ones at the table, that issues and needs beyond our own must be addressed. Thomas Merton has argued that the paradox of both faith and ethics is the need to lose ourselves (in others) in order to find ourselves.

There are no litmus tests to prove the validity of ethical norms and claims. When our founding fathers unanimously endorsed the Declaration of Independence in 1776, theirs was

Notes

Prologue

[page 2, line 24] moral engagement. John Hendry, *Between En[...]* (New York: Oxford University Press, 2004).

[page 4, line 3] ". . . ourselves on purpose." Brian J. Mahan, *Fo[...] Purpose* (San Francisco: Jossey-Bass, 2002).

[page 5, line 21] their respective disciplines. Frederick Coplesto[n] *Philosophy*, vol. 6 (London: Burns and Ordes, 1960), 181–2[...]

[page 7, line 11] ". . . a universal law." Immanuel Kant, *Foundatio[ns] of Morals*, translated by Lewis White Beck (Indianapolis: Bubb[...]

[page 7, line 23] ". . . for one, for all?" Ronald M. Green, "'Everyb[...] Reply to Richard DeGeorge," *Business Ethics Quarterly* 1, no. 2[...]

[page 8, line 7] ". . . as a means only." Kant, *Foundations*, 47.

[page 8, line 27] ". . . Judaism and Christianity." Beck quoted in Kan[...]

[page 10, line 1] can be generated. Green, "'Everybody's Doing It,[...]

Chapter 1

[page 15, line 9] his outlook on life. Paul Strathern, *Socrates in 90[...]* (Chicago: Ivan R. Dee, 1997), 19.

[page 15, line 20] ground under our feet. Christopher Phillips, *Soc[...]* (New York: W.W. Norton, 2001), 2, 3.

[page 16, line 24] ". . . is not worth living." Plato, *The Apology*, in *[...] Dialogues of Plato*, edited by Edith Hamilton and Huntington C[...] (New York: Pantheon Books, 1961), 16–23.

dependent on our ability to stand outside t[...]
on the choices we make as to what we valu[...]
and interact with others. Without some [...]
regarding human rights and responsibiliti[...]
chilling prognostication in the *Leviathan* will[...]
will be "solitary, poore, nasty, brutish, and sh[...]